The Mormon
Revelations
of Convenience

The Mormon Revelations of Convenience

Floyd McElveen

 Bethany Fellowship INC.
MINNEAPOLIS, MINNESOTA 55438

Mormon Revelations of Convenience

by Floyd McElveen

Library of Congress Catalog Card Number — 78-72945
ISBN 0-87123-385-1

Published by Bethany Fellowship, Inc.
6820 Auto Club Road, Minneapolis, Minnesota 55438

Printed in the United States of America

Dedication

To Virginia McElveen, my precious, beloved wife, and most helpful critic.

To my youngest son and his wife, Randy and Cathy McElveen, for their loving help in the Lord's work here in Bremerton, Washington, and for Randy's suggestions in analyzing the manuscript.

FLOYD CURRIE McELVEEN is a missionary with the Conservative Baptist Home Missionary Society. He spent two years and nine months in the Navy during World War II. He attended Mississippi State, Tufts College, the University of Oregon, the University of Southern Mississippi, Eastern Oregon College of Education, and Western Conservative Baptist Seminary. He has written *Christianity, Sense or Nonsense, Straight Thinking About Crooked Ideas, Will the "Saints" Go Marching In?*, and numerous religious articles for newspapers. Rev. McElveen is married, the father of three sons and a daughter, and presently lives in Bremerton, Washington, where he is starting a new church.

Acknowledgments

I would like to express my gratitude to my many friends, such as Marvin Cowan and the Tanners, who shared freely with me certain facts regarding Mormonism. Thanks to Olaf John for helping organize and sharpen up this work.

I am grateful, too, for several fleeting hours Harry Ropp spent with me, approximately two years ago, sharing his burden for Mormons to come to know the biblical Christ. He was killed in a plane crash just recently, to the sorrow of many.

Finally, many thanks to those who wrote to me concerning my last book on Mormonism, *Will the "Saints" Go Marching In?* This, and Mormons who accepted Christ and came out of Mormonism, encouraged me to write this book.

Foreword

In light of the recent revelation given to the Mormon Church through its living prophet in which blacks are now permitted to enter the priesthood, the whole subject of Mormon revelations needs to be examined.

Floyd McElveen undertakes such a task in this book in which he begins by analyzing the context and situation in which some of these changes by revelation took place. In doing so, he discovers that these changes seem to have occurred out of convenience and expediency because of the situation more than anything else.

But beyond the situation is also an extremely limited view of God in Mormon theology which provides the basis for such changes. Mormons believe that while there are many gods, there is one god with whom we have to do—a god who, like the other gods in Mormonism, is a part of the evolutive process. Obviously, as such, how could he be greater than the process? He is nothing more than a glorified man, still progressing in his godhood. As such, truth must be relative to his development and to the progress or situation of the universe of which he is a part. What absolute basis can such a god give for truth, morality, etc.?

The changing revelations led to such a limited and small view of God, and that is the god which Mormons have accepted. But sadly, in doing so, they have rejected the great and almighty God of the Bible and the salvation which He offers full and free in Jesus Christ.

I fully share Floyd McElveen's concern in reaching Mormons for Jesus Christ, and in loving fashion I believe he has revealed in the book the deficiencies of Mormon revelations and theology, and has clearly presented the true Gospel of Jesus Christ for all to consider.

James Bjornstad, Assoc. Prof. of Philosophy and Theology at Northeastern Bible College, Essex Fells, New Jersey

Preface

In June 1978, the Mormon Church issued a statement that by divine revelation it is now free to accept blacks into the priesthood.

I believe it is important to look carefully at this new Mormon revelation. The revelation which abolishes the curse forbidding entrance of black men into the Mormon priesthood may have been a surprise to some. But this new revelation fits into a pattern—a pattern suggesting that Mormon leaders are able to whip up a revelation whenever it is socially and politically convenient to do so.

The question then arises: what is revelation from God and what is not? Are there any tests which might guide us in judging what is authentic and what is spurious? Or are all their declarations given in the name of revelation acceptable?

In this book I plan to show that Mormon revelations are simply revelations of convenience, that they are not of God but of men; and that all spiritual truth that needs to be revealed to mankind has been revealed in the Holy Bible.

But I wish to write in the love of Christ. With all my heart, with all my soul, with whatever small skill I possess, I wish to reach Mormons for the Lord Jesus Christ. And to that end I dedicate these pages.

Floyd McElveen
August, 1978

Contents

Chapter 1

The Founder of the Mormon Faith

Before we look at the Mormon revelations of convenience, let's briefly review their beginnings. The Church of Jesus Christ of the Latter-Day Saints (the official designation of the Mormons) had its origin in the life of Joseph Smith (1805-1844). Smith grew up in the vicinity of Palmyra, New York. His childhood and teenage years were spent in the atmosphere of the frontier revivals—revivals that gave birth to not only a resurgence of faith but to a variety of new religious sects as well. Palmyra was the center of what the circuit-riding preachers called the "burnt over" district. One revival after another had swept through the area, leaving behind a people scattered, emotionally exhausted, and ripe for some religious instruction that would give direction to the new enthusiasm.

Teachers did appear. William Miller proclaimed that Jesus would appear on earth in March of 1843. John Humphrey Noyes taught that the millennium had already begun and gathered people into a community based on religious communism and free love. A man named Matthias strode from city to city brandishing a sword and a seven-foot ruler, shouting that he had come to redeem the world. And old Jemima Wilkinson preached that she was the Christ returned in the human form of a woman.

The Smith family was deeply involved in the religious revivalism and in the turmoil over new teaching. But the conflicting claims of the preachers confused young Joseph. Finally he went away by himself into the woods to seek an answer directly from God concerning the correct doctrines. According to Smith, his prayers were answered by a vision in which God and Jesus Christ instructed him to await further revelation.

Later Joseph testifies to an encounter with an angel named Moroni who led him to a site near Palmyra where he dug from the ground some golden plates. The plates, Joseph said, contained messages which revealed a history of the lost tribes of ancient Israel. The lost tribes, left to wander after the Northern Kingdom of Israel had been ravaged by the Assyrians in 721 B.C., had migrated to the North American continent before the birth of Christ. Called the Nephites and the Lamanites, these tribes received a special visit from Christ following His resurrection. His visit brought about the establishment of the true church of Jesus Christ in America, according to the plates.

But the Lamanites, ancestors of the American Indians, had become unfaithful and eventually they defeated the faithful Nephites. All the Nephites were killed except their leader, Mormon, and his son, Moroni. Mormon wrote their history upon the plates, using the language of ancient Egypt, and instructed Moroni to bury them until a prophet should be appointed to bring about the truth of God once again to His people.

Joseph Smith understood his task to be to translate the plates that he found. To do so he was given translating spectacles by the angel. The stone spectacles deciphered the hieroglyphics for Joseph (a remarkable achievement since scholars in Europe and America had not yet cracked the Egyptian symbol system and alphabet). Smith wrote the message down and published *The Book of Mormon* in 1830.

Smith and his followers pointed to *The Book of Mormon* as revelation additional to the Bible. The new revelation, they maintained, answered all of the pressing questions raised by the disputing sects of the time. *The Book of Mormon* stressed the free will of man, the free grace of God, and baptism as necessary for the forgiveness of sins. It rejected the baptism of infants and set out a complicated system of church government. But a major doctrine was the presentation of America as the Promised Land. America was that area of the world in which God would establish His kingdom on earth.

Followers of Joseph Smith considered their calling to be the building of "Zion" in America. Palestine, Israel, was no longer considered to be the center of God's activity. The American continent was now God's concern. Further revelations to Joseph maintained that even the Garden of Eden had been located on the American continent, somewhere in Missouri. Moreover, Smith received the message that there were many other worlds in this universe, many gods and many people making progress toward becoming gods.

The additional revelations designated Joseph Smith as the first elder of the restored church of Jesus Christ. With this position came authority to legislate doctrines through the reception of continuing messages from God. The position as first elder and receiver of revelations served Joseph well in subsequent years when inspired words from him could help resolve the storms of controversy that raged among his followers concerning issues of race and polygamy.

Joseph's new church grew with amazing speed. Many were ready and eager to accept Smith's peepstone glasses as a means for settling doctrinal disagreements. The name the group took was the Church of Jesus Christ of Latter-Day Saints, preaching that it was the true church now restored to its original teaching.

But opposition to Smith and his claims of revelations did begin to grow in the New York region. As a result the Mormons began a series of westward movements. The group moved first to Kirtland, Ohio. But then in 1837 Smith hastily moved to Independence, Missouri, in order to avoid legal action stemming from his financial dealings which the state of Ohio considered fraudulent. Smith's revelations cleared him of the legal charges to the satisfaction of his followers but not to the satisfaction of the authorities.

But Independence, Missouri, provided no rest for the Mormons. And another move was made to Nauvoo, Illinois, in 1839, with Joseph once again fleeing state prosecutors.

In Nauvoo the Mormons found security and peace for a time. Joseph continued to receive messages. He introduced the doctrine of the plurality of gods. Then he received a message condoning and encouraging polygamy. Smith taught that marriage was contracted for both time and eternity. Though St. Paul taught that in heaven there would be no marriage or giving in marriage, Joseph insisted that such conditions would not apply to his saints. In heaven a saint would not only have the wives and children sealed to him on earth, but the prerogative of procreating more, until, "the result of our endless union would be offspring as numerous as the stars of heaven. . . ."

Though Joseph's doctrines about polygamy were kept secret from unbelievers and even from some of the faithful, manuscript records suggest that Joseph may have had as many as fifty wives. A less secret doctrine was the teaching about exaltation. Joseph had revealed to him that men can become exalted to the status of gods. Joseph taught that "God himself was once as we are now, and is an exalted man." Ahead of every man there stretches an opportunity for progress to the point of attaining godhood.

But trouble with the authorities continued. And Joseph Smith met his end at the hands of an angry mob while he was confined in a jail at Carthage, Illinois. The majority of Mormons fled the area and headed west under the leadership of Brigham Young. They finally settled in the basin of the Great Salt Lake in Utah. Salt Lake City was established as a city for Mormons. And by 1870 they numbered over 140,000.

But a dissident group remained behind under the leadership of young Joseph Smith. Young Joseph and his group came to be called the Reorganized Church of Jesus Christ of Latter-Day Saints. After a time he also was able to come up with some revelations to establish his credibility as a "living prophet." Eventually the Reorganized church went back to Independence, Missouri, where young Joseph and later his son Frederick did their best to recapture the spirit of former times.

Those who followed Brigham Young to Salt Lake City continued to practice polygamy. In the isolation of the Great Basin there were few unbelievers to criticize or prosecute. Polygamy for a time became an eminently respectable practice: the number of wives a man possessed symbolized the intensity of his faith.

Yet pressure from an aroused American public did develop when Utah began requesting statehood from the U.S. Congress. For three decades authorities attempted to legislate polygamy out of existence in Mormon territory. Finally in 1890 the fourth president, Wilford Woodruff, in a manifesto intended to win both statehood and peace, renounced the practice of plural marriage while retaining the principle as an ideal. An embarrassed Mormon leadership produced another revelation that conveniently reinterpreted and set aside polygamy, Joseph Smith's last great revelation.

In the next chapter we will look at those revelations more closely.

Chapter 2

Joseph Smith and the Revelations Concerning Polygamy

The pattern of conflicting revelations within Mormonism is apparent from a look at the controversial doctrine and practice of polygamy among Mormons. Joseph Smith's revelation in the *Book of Mormon* expressly forbade plural marriages. And his revelation recorded in the 1835 edition of *Doctrine and Covenants* reinforced the teachings against fornication, adultery and polygamy.

The peepstone spectacles allowed Joseph to see the golden plates saying, "And now it came to pass that the people of Nephi, under the reign of the second king, began to grow hard in their hearts, and indulge themselves somewhat in wicked practices, such as like David of old desiring many wives and concubines, and also Solomon, his son" (*Book of Mormon*, Jacob 1:15). Here Joseph Smith says that God declared the having of many wives to be wicked. And again the text says, "Behold, David and Solomon truly had many wives and concubines, which thing was an abomination before me, saith the Lord" (Jacob 2:24).

The plain fact is that the *Book of Mormon* clearly and

forthrightly forbids the taking of more than one wife. Such practice is considered an abomination in the eyes of God. "Behold, the Lamanites, your brethren, whom ye hate because of their filthiness and the cursing which hath come upon their skins, are more righteous than you; for they have not forgotten the commandment of the Lord, which was given to our fathers—that they should have as it were one wife, and concubines they should have none, and there should not be whoredoms committed among them" (Jacob 3:5).

Yet in only a few years, Joseph Smith said he received another revelation from God *commanding* polygamy. *Doctrine and Covenants* records the new, contradictory revelation as occurring on July 12, 1843. Historical records indicate that at least 27 women were secretly married to Joseph Smith prior to the new revelation. Some of the women gave sworn testimony that they had been married to, and had sexual relations with, the prophet Joseph Smith (*Covenants* 132:61, 62). Both Mormon and non-Mormon historians agree that these adulterous relationships were established before the revelation of 1843.

Joseph's immediate concern in getting a new revelation seems to have been to pacify his first wife Emma. Poor Emma had been listening to a lot of gossip concerning Joseph and his friendship with young girls and other married women. And she didn't like the gossip. So Joseph managed to put together a new revelation. Notice how Joseph sets the stage for the revelation that will contradict what had been previously revealed.

> For behold, I reveal unto you a new and *everlasting* covenant: and if ye abide not in that covenant, then are ye damned: for no one can reject this covenant and be permitted to enter into my glory (*Doctrine and Covenants,* sec. 132:4).

But the new revelation contradicts not only Joseph's own previous revelations, it contradicts the Bible as well. Smith said, "Abraham received concubines, and they bore him children: and it was accounted unto him for righteousness. . ." (*Doctrine and Covenants,* 132:37a). But the Bible says about Abraham, "And he believed the Lord; and he reckoned it to him as righteousness" (Genesis 15:6). The new revelation contradicts the earlier one which said that sexual relations with many women were abominable and wicked. And the new revelation distorts in a malicious way the Bible account of Abraham's righteousness. The Bible says Abraham was righteous because he believed God.

But Joseph's new revelation continues:

> David's wives and concubines were given unto him of me, by the hand of Nathan, my servant, and others of the prophets who had the keys of this power: and in none of these things did he sin against me save in the case of Uriah and his wife. . . .

And now Joseph is ready for poor Emma who must be consoled and comforted.

> And let mine handmaid, Emma Smith, receive all those that have been given unto my servant Joseph. . . . And I command mine handmaid, Emma Smith, to abide and cleave unto my servant Joseph and to none else. But if she will not abide this commandment she shall be destroyed, saith the Lord; for I am the Lord thy God, and will destroy her if she abide not in my law (*Doctrine and Covenants* 132:54).

There is little comfort there for Emma. She must accept polygamy or face the threat of destruction. Yet she must have wondered with us which revelation to receive as authentic, the *Book of Mormon* or the new revelation of convenience. Or do you suppose that she might have begun to suspect that neither were authentic revelations from God? Can God be the author of such confusion and contradiction?

Mormons had been under heavy fire for some years because of rumors circulating in the Nauvoo, Illinois, territory about plural marriages. The church officials consistently denied the rumors, insisting that the *Book of Mormon* condemned polygamy, adultery and fornication. The Mormon newspaper, *Millennial Star,* had insisted that despite rumors, polygamy was against Mormon teaching.

> But for the information of those who may be assailed by those foolish tales about two wives, we would say that no such principle ever existed among the Latter Day Saints, and never will: this is well known to all who are acquainted with our books and actions, the *Book of Mormon, Doctrine and Covenants:* and also all our periodicals are very strict and explicit on that subject, indeed far more so than the Bible (*Millennial Star* III, 74).

I do not in any way want to be harsh or unfair. But it seems clear that the revelations, explanations, denials, and threats are nothing more than phoney devices used by Joseph Smith and his cohorts as a way to get what they wanted. They lusted after many women. So they turned up with a revelation allowing them to have as many women as they wanted.

Yet Mormon denials of polygamy are numerous. Notice this statement by John Taylor in 1850.

> We are accused here of polygamy, and actions the most indelicate, obscene, and disgusting, such that none but a corrupt and depraved heart could have contrived. These things are too outrageous to admit of belief. . . . I shall content myself by reading our views of chastity and marriage from a work published by us, containing some of the articles of our Faith.

Doctrine and Covenants, page 330: "Inasmuch as this church of Jesus Christ has been reproached with the crime of fornication and polygamy, we declare that we believe that one man should have one wife, and one woman but one husband, except in case of death, when either is at liberty to marry again."

This statement of John Taylor's was published by the Mormon apostle Orson Pratt in the 1851 edition of his *Works* from a tract written by John Taylor. At the time, however, Taylor had six wives of his own, Lonora Canon, Elizabeth Haigham, Jane Ballantyne, Mary Ann Oakley, Sophia Whitaker, and Harriet Whitaker. Taylor was later to become the third president and living prophet of the Mormon church.

I hesitate to label this sort of thing as it should be labelled. I love the Mormons too much to needlessly hurt or insult them. And I want Mormons to turn from these contradictory and abominable revelations. I long that they would turn to the biblical Christ.

Yet it is upon a foundation of contradictory and fabricated revelations that Mormonism is built. It is bad enough that Joseph Smith asked people to believe that he could translate Egyptian hieroglyphics by peering through some pieces of stone. For him to then heap more confusion upon people by his continuing pronouncements that simply served his own carnal desires is an abuse too heinous to let pass.

In short, this is what we have: Joseph Smith in his revelation as found in *The Book of Mormon* forbade polygamy. And in the 1835 version of *Doctrine and Covenants,* he reiterated his stand against polygamy in response to charges from unbelievers that Mormons practiced fornication and plural marriage. But then Joseph claimed to have had another revelation commanding polygamy in 1843 and saying that it was a new and everlasting covenant.

Given the fact of accusations from both within and without the church concerning Mormon leaders living in adulterous relations with a number of women, it seems that Joseph's new revelation was just a convenient device to make right what all knew to be wrong. If after years of marriage to a woman somewhat older than himself, Joseph yearned for both variety and youth, he knew by now that as a prophet it was easier to change marriage laws than to deliberately break them. So, Joseph fetched himself up another revelation.

The conclusive proof that the revelations were not from God is that they hopelessly contradict one another. They make God out to be a liar, a breaker of His own moral law. The very best that can be said for the revelations concerning marriage to many women is that they are confusing. But, my friends, God is not the author of confusion!

Chapter 3

More Mormon Revelations Concerning Polygamy

Mormons after Joseph Smith were firmly entrenched by practice, prophecy, and proclamation in polygamy. Smith claimed that God's revelation to him concerning plural marriages was an *everlasting* covenant, and those who did not *abide* in it were *damned*. Other Mormons, such as Apostle Orson Hyde and Apostle Orson Pratt, declared that Jesus himself was polygamous. He had been married at Cana of Galilee, it was said. Mary, Martha and others were also His wives. God, too, according to Brigham Young, had sexual intercourse with many wives.

But I do not want to deal with this strange and blasphemous doctrine here. Yet I must not fail to mention that Brigham Young said in the *Journal of Discourses,* where 363 of his sermons are recorded, "I have never yet preached a sermon and sent it out to the children of men that they may not call Scripture. Let me have the privilege of correcting a sermon, and it is as good Scripture as they deserve" (*Journal of Discourses.* Liverpool, England: F. D. and S. W. Richards, 1854. Reprinted edition, Salt Lake City, 1966. vol. 13, page 95).

This is an important statement, for it prevents agile Mormons of today from dodging the impact of Brigham Young's statements. He considered them to be revelation, on par with Scripture. And to deny his statements is to deny Mormonism.

To note what Brigham Young says: "The only men who become gods, even the sons of god, are those who enter into polygamy" (*Journal of Discourses,* vol. 11, page 269. See also vol. 3, page 266.). If this is so, then no modern-day Mormon can ever be exalted! Worse yet, for the Mormons, Joseph Smith declared that God had given polygamy as an everlasting covenant. And "all who do not abide in that covenant are damned" (*Doctrine and Covenants,* 132:4). The Mormon revelations of early authorities made polygamy mandatory. This conclusion is about as sure and solid as any conclusion can be.

Estimates on how many Mormons practiced polygamy vary from 2% to 16% of the Mormon population. These estimates come from Mormon sources. In any event, thousands were involved in polygamy. Even today, Wallace Turner, writing for the *New York Times* newspaper, stated,

> The problem of polygamy—for half a century a cardinal principle of Mormonism—has taken a number of members out of the church. One expert estimates that as many as 30,000 men, women, and children live in families in which polygamy is practiced. . . . Many live in and near Salt Lake City. Hundreds are concentrated in an isolated Arizona town, Colorado City. Others are scattered through the mountain West and in Mexico (*New York Times,* December 27, 1965).

Bills against polygamy were introduced into the United

States Congress in 1860, 1866, and 1869. The Edmunds Bill passed and finally became law. The law disenfranchised all polygamists and imposed heavy fines and imprisonment on them. The response from Mormons to this federal legislation is interesting.

Brigham Young's First Counselor, Heber C. Kimball, said, "The principle of the plurality of wives never will be done away . . ." (*Desert News*, November 7, 1855). And again, "Some quietly listen to those who speak against the Lord's servants, against His anointed, against the plurality of wives, and against almost every principle that God has revealed. Such persons have half a dozen devils with them all the time. You might as well deny Mormonism and turn away from it, as to oppose the plurality of wives" (*Journal of Discourses*, vol. 5, page 203).

In the *Millennial Star* newspaper Kimball declared, "It would be as easy for the United States to build a tower to remove the sun, as to remove polygamy, or the church and kingdom of God" (Volume 28, page 190). And Orson Pratt stated, "Those who reject this principle [polygamy] reject their own salvation, they shall be damned" (Apostle Orson Pratt, *Journal of Discourses,* volume 17, pages 224-225).

George Q. Cannon boldly asserted, "If plural marriage be Divine, as the Latter-Day Saints say it is, no power on earth can suppress it" (*Journal of Discourses,* volume 20, page 276). Apostle Orson Hyde declared that polygamy is "the very principle that will break in pieces the power that would set it aside" (*Ibid.,* volume 13, page 183).

Wilford Woodruff, in 1869, said,

If we were to do away with polygamy . . . then we must do away with prophets and Apostles, with revelation and the gifts and graces of the Gospel, and finally give up our religion altogether and turn sectari-

ans and do as the world does. . . . We just can't do
that, for God has commanded us to build up his kingdom . . . and we shall obey Him in days to come as we
have in days past (*Ibid.,* volume 13, page 166).

The *Millennial Star*, the newspaper reflecting the opin-
ions of Mormon leaders on national issues, said in 1865,

All this Congress demands of the people of Utah. It
asks the repudiation of their entire religious practice
today; and inasmuch as polygamy is, in Mormon belief, the basis of the condition of a future life, it asks
them to give up their hopes of salvation here-
after. . . . There is no half-way house. The childish
babble about another revelation is only an evidence
how half informed men can talk . . . (*Millennial Star,*
October 28, 1865).

Mormons began to be put on trial for practicing polygamy, and their property was confiscated. Pressure mounted.
But all resistance to government pressure and all the en-
couragement to follow God in polygamy ended when in 1890
Wilford Woodruff, President and Living Prophet, spoke a
new word from God. The new word was that polygamy was
not essential to exaltation. The word said that men may be
exalted to sonship without having many wives, that previous declarations and revelations about the necessity of polygamy were now not to be followed. Mormons were asked to
believe that God had changed His mind. But not only had
He changed His mind, He was now contradicting himself.
Or is there another explanation? Could it be that the many
prophets speaking for polygamy in the past had been hood-
winking the faithful Mormon brethren all along?

The everlasting covenant of polygamy was now declared
null and void. But again a pattern to Mormon revelation
emerges. Pressure—social or political or financial—always
produces new revelations. And the new ones contradict the
old ones.

Chapter 4

The Black Man in Mormon Revelation

Mormons claim that God put a curse on the Negro race. Joseph Smith in the *Book of Mormon* asserted that God cursed a white people because of their sins by making "a skin of blackness come upon them." The Lamanites, forerunners of today's American Indians, were also made dark as "a curse upon them because of their transgression." Another excerpt from *The Book of Mormon* says, "And it came to pass that I beheld, after they had dwindled in unbelief they became a dark and loathsome, and a filthy people, full of idleness and all manner of abominations."

According to *The Book of Mormon,* dark or black skin is a sign of God's curse upon a whole race. Conversely, white skin testifies to God's blessing.

Later, in *Pearl of Great Price,* Joseph Smith extended the penalities of the curse upon blacks by forbidding them access to the priesthood and exaltation to the highest heaven. The story of Joseph's translation of the *Pearl of Great Price (The Book of Abraham)* points up the absurdity of Mormon revelation. In 1835, while still living in Kirtland, Ohio, Joseph received as a visitor Michael Chandler. Chandler had been touring the country exhibiting four Egyptian mummies along with several papyri taken from some tombs in Egypt. Linguists in New York and Philadelphia had pronounced the papyri markings as authentic Egyptian, but could only guess at their meaning. Learning of Joseph's reputation as a translator, Chandler asked Joseph for a translation.

After a preliminary examination, the prophet declared one papyrus to be the writings of Abraham and the other to be the work of Joseph of Egypt. He set to work on the writings of Abraham with his peepstone glasses. The text that Joseph produced (published in 1842) told a story of creation corresponding roughly to the first two chapters of Genesis. But then it took off on a flight of fresh and original fancy. Abraham, Joseph alleged, was an eminent astronomer able to penetrate all the mysteries of the universe. And the book told of the movements of the planets and the stars, their inhabitants, and their proximity to the throne of God.

But the *Book of Abraham* spoke not only of the heavens, but also of the origin of the races on earth. The story of the curse of Noah upon his son Ham is repeated, and Ham's son Canaan is doomed to life as a "servant of servants." Pharaoh, first ruler of Egypt, Joseph said, was the son of Egyptus, daughter of Ham. All Egyptians, therefore, inherited the curse of black skin. But the curse was even more complicated than the doom pronounced upon Ham. The war in heaven between the followers of Lucifer and Jehovah (told in Ezekiel) had not ended simply in the followers of Lucifer being thrown out of heaven. A third group of spirits which had attempted to remain neutral in the conflict were required to inhabit human bodies and to share in the accursed lineage of Canaan. These neutral spirits which had in cowardice waited to join with the winning side in the heavenly battle were made the Negro or African race.

The *Book of Abraham* left Joseph open to the ridicule of future scholars. Unlike the Golden plates, which had been whisked back into heaven where no one could see them again, the mummies and papyri were kept on exhibit in both Kirtland and Nauvoo. After Smith's death the papyri were lost for a time. But a manuscript containing the Egyptian hieroglyphics and Smith's translation was discovered and given to the Latter-Day Saints by the New York Metropolitan Museum of Art in 1967.

The half-dozen scholars asked to examine the manuscript hieroglyphics agree that the document is an ordinary funeral document such as can be found on thousands of Egyptian graves. One scholar examining the manuscript was Dee Jay Nelson, a Mormon priest and Egyptologist of note. He examined the hieroglyphics and Smith's alleged translation and declared the translation to be a fraud. Nelson sought the opinion of other scholars for a check on his conclusions. They confirmed his judgment. (Nelson's correspondence with LDS authorities is provided in Appendix 1.)

The *Book of Abraham* is judged by Egyptologists to be a fraud, Joseph Smith a false prophet. Mormon scholar Dr. Hugh Nibley, though publicly admitting that he is not an Egyptologist, nevertheless tried to talk around the implications of a fraudulent book as a basis for Mormon faith and doctrine. His explanation amounts to a smokescreen of imprecise theological jargon. And though Nelson resigned his priesthood and membership in the LDS church, and though other scholars confirmed his findings about the Smith "translation," the curse on the Negro by the Mormon church remained. Apostle Bruce R. McConkie states the doctrine in these words:

Those who were less valiant in pre-existence and who

thereby had certain spiritual restrictions imposed upon them during mortality are known to us as the Negroes. Such spirits are sent to earth through the lineage of Cain, the mark put upon him for his rebellion against God and his murder of Abel being a black skin.

McConkie also writes,

Negroes in this life are denied the priesthood; under no circumstances can they hold this delegation of authority from the Almighty. The gospel message of salvation is not carried affirmatively to them. . . . Negroes are not equal with other races where the receipt of certain spiritual blessings are concerned (*Mormon Doctrine*, 476-477).

How long was the curse on the Negro to last? Living Prophets and authorities differ in their answers. Mormon Mark E. Petersen claimed that the Negro might be able to enter the celestial glory as a servant. But Living Prophet and President Brigham Young wrote,

I had rather see a colored man, who is my friend here, sent to Washington, because he is not capable of receiving the priesthood, and can never reach the highest celestial glory of the kingdom of God (Salt Lake Tribune, October 5, 1884).

Another view is given by Mormon writer John L. Lund in *The Church and the Negro.* He says, "Brigham Young revealed that the Negroes will not receive the priesthood until a great while after the second advent of Jesus Christ, whose coming will usher in a millennium of peace."

Again Lund states, "The Negroes will not be allowed to hold the priesthood during mortality, in fact, not until after the resurrection of all Adam's children. . . . This will not happen until after the thousand years of Christ's reign on earth."

In the same writing Lund said that the church would not have a new revelation on the issue of the Negroes even though there were groups in the church, as well as social pressure from outside the church, to change the standard doctrine. "All the social, political, and governmental pressure in the world is not going to change what God has decreed to be," Lund said.

The *Book of Abraham* taught that the first Pharaoh of Egypt was a descendant of Ham and a blood relation of the Canaanites. From this line of Ham sprang all the Egyptians. The curse was, therefore, upon all the Egyptians. Pharaoh himself was "of that lineage by which he could not have the right of priesthood."

The Mormon faithful, however, declare themselves to be of the tribe of Manasseh and Ephraim. When Joseph, the youngest son of Jacob (Israel), was in Egypt he was given a wife who was the daughter of an Egyptian priest. This story appears in Genesis chapter 41. His Egyptian wife was named Asenath. She bore him two sons, Manasseh and Ephraim.

The conclusion is clear: by their own theology and genealogical calculations, most Mormon males are ineligible to hold their own priesthood! They are of the blood of the cursed Egyptians.

A Mormon missionary in Bremerton, Washington, when confronted with this evidence, said that, after all, there were both white and black Egyptians. And the curse was only upon the black Egyptians. But the *Book of Abraham* says that the curse is upon *all* Egyptians. One could not possibly be a descendant of Manasseh and Ephraim and not have any Egyptian blood in him. Yet, one *drop* of the blood of Cain disqualified a man from the priesthood according to Brigham Young and Wilford Woodruff. And who knows whether that blood is "black" or "white" blood? Another contradiction in Mormon theology appears. Something must be wrong with these revelations!

So, it is possible to see some presssure building up behind the scenes to make necessary a new revelation regarding the Negro race. When Joseph Smith "received" his revelations, slavery still existed in much of the United States. The strange notion of a curse on millions of Negroes may have been easier to accept in those days when all around people could see the black man in chains. But by holding to the doctrine, the Mormon church found itself desperately out of step with the times.

The civil rights movement of the sixties hit the Mormon church hard for its discriminatory policies. Eight Negroes boycotted a track meet with Brigham Young University. And other universities took the hint and refused to compete with BYU so long as it maintained its anti-Negro doctrine and attitudes.

But it is not easy to turn around one hundred years of discriminatory thinking. Joseph Fielding Smith who became the tenth President of the Mormon church in January of 1970, declared in *The Way to Perfection* (1931), that "Not only was Cain called upon to suffer, but because of his wickedness he became the father of an *inferior* race. A curse was placed upon him and that curse has been continued through his lineage and must do so while time endures."

Yet, sure enough, a new revelation did emerge from the embattled leadership. In June, 1978, what should God suddenly decide about the "everlasting" curse? That it was null and void!

"ALL WORTHY MALE MEMBERS OF THE MORMON CHURCH MAY NOW HOLD THE PRIESTHOOD, REGARDLESS OF RACE OR COLOR."

How revelation does change! We are happy that there may now be less bigotry and racism in the Mormon church. But we are sad because this change may encourage some blacks to join the church. They should not! The contradictory revelations are simply not trustworthy. Who knows what might appear from the mouth of the prophets next?

Look what Brigham Young said:

> The First Presidency, the Twelve, High Council, Bishopprick, and all Elders of Israel, suppose we summon them to appear here and declare that it is right to mingle our seed with the black race of Cain, that they shall come in with us and be partakers with us of all the blessings God has given us. On that very day and hour we should do so the Priesthood is taken from the Church and Kingdom and God leaves us to our fate. The moment we consent to mingle with the seed of Cain the Church must go to destruction. . . . We should receive the curse which has been placed upon the seed of Cain, and nevermore be numbered with the children of Adam who are heirs to the Priesthood until that curse be removed. (An unpublished address by Brigham Young, in the Mormon Church Archives, Manuscript D, No. 1234. BX.48, Folder 3, Feb. 5, 1852. *Supplied by Marvin Cowan.*)

Where does this new development leave the Mormon church but with another revelation of convenience? Might we expect a new revelation concerning the status of women if the Equal Rights Amendment is ratified?

Chapter 5

The Fruits of Mormon Revelation

This chapter is the most difficult of all to write. I pray that I might write it in the love of Christ. And yet it must be written in such a way that Mormons might see that they have been deceived by spurious revelation. My experience tells me that to win Mormons to Christ it is necessary first that Mormons become disenchanted with Mormonism. Mormon revelation presents to them an entirely different Jesus than the Jesus of the Bible. But it is the Jesus of the Bible that saves, enlightens, and brings forgiveness.

Fundamental, evangelical, Bible-believing, born-again Christians, by the tens of millions, for hundreds of years—simple saints and brilliant scholars alike—have agreed that the Bible is complete. New prophets are not necessary to bring new revelation in this age of the Church. By the word "prophet," I mean one who supernaturally transmits revelations added to scripture. The word "prophet" literally means, from the Greek, "one who speaks for"—that is, one who speaks for God. But God has already, "in these last days spoken unto us by his Son, whom he hath appointed

heir of all things, by whom also he made the worlds. . ."
(Hebrews 1:2).

The mark of a cult in almost all cases is the claim to
some new revelation in addition to scripture. A cult always
wants to add to scripture. And they make the additional
revelation the basis for their claim that always follows on
the heels of the revelation. That claim is that they are the
one true church. These two signs, then, mark the cults: a
claim to new revelation additional to scripture and the
claim to be the one true church outside of which there is no
salvation (or a lesser, second-class salvation).

But upon what grounds do Christians rest when they say
that revelation has ended, that the Bible is complete? First,
Christ promised that He by the Holy Spirit would lead
His people and His church into all the truth (John 16:13).
Second, the Old Testament through the prophet, priest, and
the ritual sacrifices foretold and prepared the way for the
coming of the Messiah, the Christ. The New Testament,
containing the new covenant, fulfills the old and shows that
Jesus Christ has come. The New Testament recounts in
great detail His life, His miracles, His death and His resurrection to show that all is fully revealed.

Paul's letter to the Hebrews, quoted earlier, says,

> God, who at sundry times and in diverse manners
> spake in time past unto the fathers by the prophets,
> hath in these last days spoken unto us by his Son,
> whom he hath appointed heir of all things, by whom
> also he made the worlds. Who, being the brightness of
> his glory, and the express image of his person, and
> upholding all things by the word of his power, when
> he had by himself purged our sins, sat down on the
> right hand of the Majesty on high. . . . (Hebrews
> 1:1-3).

Paul goes on to tell of the replacing of the old covenant

with the new covenant. Both covenants, however, entailed a revelation from God. Holy men of God, the prophets and apostles, spoke and wrote what God revealed to them.

Now it is important to note that Jesus never indicated that revelation of the old covenant was inadequate or erroneous. His use of it testified to its adequacy. Jesus and the apostles and prophets of the New Testament era spoke and wrote of the new covenant. The new covenant, like the old, was fully and adequately explained. The New Testament is the new covenant spelled out. There will *never* be any *better* or *newer* covenant. That is why this covenant is called the "everlasting covenant" in Hebrews 13:20.

Christians, who base their certainty of salvation upon their experience of forgiveness through Jesus Christ (and not upon membership in any institution calling itself the one true church), wait for the second coming of the Lord Jesus. That truth has been fully revealed. After He comes, there will certainly be no need of further revelation. We will be with Him and be like Him!

Therefore, the old covenant is given. The new, everlasting covenant is also given. There is no gap, no emptiness, no need for anything new. In fact, the New Testament warns,

> I testify unto every man that heareth the words of the prophecy of this book, If any man shall add unto these things, God shall add unto him the plagues that are written in this book: and if any man shall take away from the words of the book of this prophecy, God shall take away his part out of the book of life, and out of the holy city, and from the things which are written in this book (Revelation 12:18, 19).

This severe warning against subtracting from or adding to the Word of God is found not only in the book of Revelation. A similar warning is given in Deuteronomy 4:2. So we have near the beginning of the Bible and again at the end the warning that new revelation is not to be considered by believers. The Bible is complete! Mormons may answer that much new revelation was given AFTER the warning given in Deut. 4:2, which we acknowledge to be of God, and which is recorded in the Bible. Therefore, they may reason, new revelation may be given and added as Scripture AFTER the warning given in Rev. 22:18-19. However, Deut. 4:2 says, in part, "Ye shall not add unto the word which I command you . . ." not, "HAVE commanded you, or already completely given you!" Obviously, THIS warning dealt with ongoing revelation. NOT SO the more severe warning in Rev. 22:18-19. The Revelation warning clearly deals with revelation ALREADY GIVEN, already complete.

While the primary application of this warning is to the book of Revelation, it is very doubtful if we can limit the application ONLY to the book of Revelation. It is a certain fact that an all-knowing God, who knows the end from the beginning, knew that under His promised guidance, the book of Revelation would be placed as the LAST book of the Bible. It is simple too much to ask us to believe that it is mere coincidence that the most drastic warning in the Bible concerning adding to its words or prophecies, would be on the LAST page of the LAST chapter of the LAST book of the Bible, by the LAST prophet, unless God wanted this warning to apply to MORE than just the book of Revelation! Rather, He stamped this book, both Revelation and the Bible, as His last prophecies for the Church Age. The Bible is complete.

The proof of this as the correct interpretation is in the irrefutable historical fact that NO prophet since the Bible was completed has ever passed the 100% accuracy test of Deut. 18:20-22, required as an absolute necessary proof of a man being a prophet of God. ALL who claimed to be prophets since the Bible was completed have had prophecies that failed, proving them to be false prophets! There is NO new revelation from God! The book of Revelation does say that in the last days two witnesses will appear and prophesy. But it is not said that they will provide new information or additional information. Rather, they are witnesses, and witnesses give testimony. This is to occur after the Church has gone to be with the Lord Jesus Christ. The Church age will have ended.

There is no revelation left to give. The old covenant and the new covenant are fully given. God did not forget anything. The book of Revelation provides information concerning the end of the Church age, the great tribulation, the millennium, and the consummation of all things. It is strange that some would feel a need for more revelation!

But for all who appear as prophets to give new revelations, Deuteronomy 18:22 gives a rule for determining their authenticity:

> When a prophet speaketh in the name of the Lord, if the thing follow not, nor come to pass, that is the thing which the Lord hath not spoken, but the prophet hath spoken it presumptuously. . . .

But what of Mormon revelations? Some of the contradictions we have already seen in earlier chapters. But there are more, many more. Christ said, "By their fruits ye shall know them." Here is the fruit of Mormon prophets, quoted from the *Pearl of Great Price. The Book of Abraham*, 4:1: "And then the Lord said: Let us go down. And they went down at the beginning, and they, that is the gods, organized and formed the heavens and the earth."

The Mormon church teaches, in direct opposition to the Bible, as well as *The Book of Mormon*, that there are many gods. There are gods for many different worlds or planets. And certain Mormons may themselves become gods when their exaltation is complete.

To believe in a plurality of gods is contrary to biblical revelation. It is an affront to God. Such belief smacks of paganism, a paganism not unlike that of the Roman Empire.

To evade this charge of paganism, Mormons often say, "But we have one God with whom we have to deal." They mean that there is only one God for this world (but other gods exist for other worlds).

This answer is an evasion. The Bible says that the heaven of heavens cannot contain God! There is nowhere that God is not (Isaiah 44:8), "Have not I told thee from that time and have declared it? Ye are even my witnesses. Is there a God beside me? Yea, there is no God; I know not any."

Yet according to Joseph Smith in *Pearl of Great Price*, the gods got together and made the heavens and the earth. How then could God say that He was the one and only God, as He does repeatedly in the Bible, and that He knew of no other god? If the "gods" cooperated in making this earth, how can Mormons then say that we have only one God with whom we must deal in this world?

Mormon revelation also teaches that God was not always God, but that He was once a man. But Psalms 90:2b declares that "from everlasting to everlasting, thou art God." Joseph Smith, however, said before his congregation of believers,

> I am going to tell you how God came to be God. We have imagined and supposed that God was God from all eternity. I will refute that idea, and take away the veil, so that you may see (*Journal of Discourses*, volume 6, April 6, 1844.)

This Mormon revelation concerning God once being a man and advancing or progressing to be God, is stated this way by President Lorenzo Snow in the *Millennial Star* and Milton Hunter in the book *The Gospel Through the Ages.* "As man is, God once was; as God is man may be."

Biblical scripture answers this succinctly: "Before me there was no God formed, neither shall there be after me" (Isaiah 43:10b). The unchangeable God was never man. And there was not, is not, and never will be any other God. Men will never become gods.

Mormon revelation also leads to such ridiculous statements as this one by Prophet Brigham Young, speaking of Adam in *Journal of Discourses.* "He [Adam] is our Father and our God, and the only God with whom we have to do." For Brigham Young to say such a thing is to contradict scripture. And President and Living Prophet Spencer W. Kimball (the same no less than he who gave the new revelation about Negroes entering the church) said:

> We warn you against the dissemination of doctrines which are not according to the scriptures, and which are alleged to have been taught by some of the General Authorities of past generations. Such, for instance, is the Adam-God theory. We denounce that theory and hope that everyone will be cautioned against this and other kinds of false doctrines.

Here we have one president contradicting and denouncing the inspired teachings of another. God, my dear friends, is not the author of such confusion! Brigham Young repeated his teaching many times. This is recorded, and leading Mormons know it. Numerous Mormon writers of his time quoted him, believed him, and supported his statements. For over 50 years, Mormon records show that Mormons accepted Brigham Young's Adam-God doctrine. Brigham

Young preached on the doctrine a number of times spanning over 20 years, and we have the quotes of leading Mormons of that time to prove it. He never made any attempt to change his printed sermons about Adam being God, recorded in the *Journal of Discourses* and elsewhere, during all those years. To try to sweep it under the rug now by saying that Brigham Young was misquoted or misunderstood is simply dishonest.

Mormons also teach that Christ is the Spirit-brother of Satan. The Bible teaches, however, that Jesus Christ created all things (John 1:1-3), visible and invisible (Colossians 1:16, 17), including angels. Satan was created as an angelic being. But then he fell. Jesus was God, from everlasting (Isaiah 9:6, Micah 5:2, John 1:1) and not a created being. Mormons teach that Jesus Christ is Jehovah, a God who has earned or progressed into Godhead. Jehovah, they say, is different from Elohim, who is God the Father.

According to Mormonism, these two are (Jehovah and Elohim) one only in purpose. Allow me a few observations about this. First, this teaching contradicts the teaching that there is only one God with whom we have to deal. Joseph Smith claimed to have seen both Jesus Christ and God the Father in his first vision. Second, the Bible frequently uses words in such a way as to make Smith's conclusion absolutely impossible. One clear and simple verse is Deuteronomy 6:4b: "The Lord [Jehovah] our God [Elohim] is our Lord [Jehovah]." The literal rendering of this verse is that Jehovah our Elohim is one Jehovah. The Mormons can never become true Christians until they realize that Jesus Christ is one with the Father (not just one in purpose). In response to the disciple Phillip's request that Jesus show them the Father, Jesus said, "He that hath seen me hath seen the Father" (John 14:9b). My wife and I are one, according to

Ephesians 5:31. Nevertheless, if you see me, by no stretch of the imagination can you say that you have seen Virginia! (She's much prettier, praise the Lord!). But Jesus could say that when someone had seen Him, they HAD seen the Father, because they are one in essence, in nature, NOT just one in purpose.

The Bible says that to know Jesus is to know God, to see Jesus is to see God, to believe in Jesus is to believe in God, to honor Jesus is to honor God, to receive Jesus is to receive God, to worship Jesus is to worship God, and to hate Jesus is to hate God. God is called the First and the Last. Jesus Christ is called the First and the Last, the Alpha and Omega. Jesus forgave sin; the Bible says only God can forgive sin. Things that are said in the Old Testament about God are said in the New Testament about Jesus. The Father God is called our Savior and the Creator in the Old Testament. Jesus Christ is called our Saviour and the Creator in the New Testament. An elementary rule of logic is that things equal to the same thing are equal to each other (if A equals B and B equals C, then A equals C). Jesus is thus declared to be God.

But here are some other fruits of Mormon revelation. Joseph Smith's son, also named Joseph, was chosen by Joseph Smith to be his successor in the winter of 1843 in Nauvoo, Illinois. Joseph Smith ordained his own son, he was anointed by the patriarch Hyrum Smith, and Newell K. Whitney poured the oil upon him. Others present included two of the Twelve Apostles, John Taylor and Willard Richards. The information is available today in the plaintiffs Abstract, Temple Lot Suit. In court cases of 1880 and 1894 the Re-organized Church of Jesus Christ of Latter-Day Saints, not the group who travelled to Salt Lake City, were declared to be the true successors of Smith and entitled to the rights and properties of the church founded by Joseph Smith.

How could the prophet and President Joseph Smith have made such a crucial mistake? His declaration was another alleged revelation. If Joseph Smith was right, then Brigham Young was a false prophet leading a false church. If Joseph Smith was wrong, then he himself was a false prophet.

God's test to determine if a prophet is true or false, whether he speaks of God or not of God, is given in scripture. The passage quoted earlier from Deuteronomy 18:22 should be repeated often:

> But the prophet, which shall presume to speak a word in my name, which I have not commanded him to speak, or shall speak in the name of other gods, even that prophet shall die. And if thou say in thine heart, How shall we know the word which the Lord hath not spoken? When a prophet speaketh in the name of the Lord, if the thing follow not, nor come to pass, that is the thing which the Lord hath not spoken, but the prophet hath spoken it presumptuously: thou shalt not be afraid of him. (vv. 20-22).

This test ought to be read together with Deuteronomy 13:1-5, which says that if even something a prophet did predict came to pass, but the prophet's words led the people astray, then the prophet is a false prophet.

Let's try this test with Joseph Smith and Brigham Young. To begin with, Joseph Smith taught that the moon was inhabited. Brigham Young went him one better and taught that both the moon and the sun were inhabited (*Journal of Discourses*, volume 13, page 271). He taught that gold and silver grow like plants (volume 1, page 219). These are simply absurd statements by ignorant men. But then Brigham Young goes on to say that the blood of the

Lord Jesus Christ cannot atone for some sins, but that a man's own blood must be shed to wash away some sins (*Journal of Discourses*, volume 4, pages 53, 54). Brigham Young also said that "When the whole body is full of the Holy Ghost, he can see behind him with as much ease, without turning his head, as he can see before him. If you have not that experience you ought to have." Brigham Young also taught that Jesus Christ was "not begotten by the Holy Ghost" (*Journal of Discourses*, volume 1, pages 50, 51).

Such nonsense in the name of Christ is hardly worth a reply. But many fine people, because of a "burning feeling" or a "testimony" have bound themselves to believing such things.

One of the most embarrassing revelations of Joseph Smith is recorded in a book by one of the so-called Three Witnesses to the *Book of Mormon*. David Whitmer, in a book titled *An Address to All Believers in Christ* (Richmond, Missouri, 1887) tells how Joseph Smith received "a revelation that some of the brethren should go to Toronto, Canada, and that they would sell the copyright of *The Book of Mormon.*" The brethren went to Toronto, but their attempts to sell the copyright were fruitless. They could not sell it. They returned disillusioned, convinced that Joseph's revelations must be questionable.

When confronted with this failure, Joseph Smith quickly assured the brethren that, "Some revelations are of God; some are of men; and some revelations are of the devil." The problem with this answer is that who knows which prophecy is which? Joseph was remiss not to point out that the scriptural view is that false prophecy proves a man to be a false prophet. And the scriptural penalty is death. Read Deuteronomy 18:22-22 again!

Joseph Smith laid hands on Lyman Wright to ordain

him to the High Priesthood. Then Lyman Wright also prophesied because of the laying on of hands. "And the Spirit fell upon Lyman, and he prophesied concerning the coming of Christ. He said that there were some in the congregation that should live until the saviour should descend from heaven with a shout, with all the holy angels with Him." This is recorded in *Documentary History of the Church* by David Whitmer (volume 1, page 176, dated March 6, 1831). It was a false prophecy by a Mormon High Priest, and Joseph Smith was party to it.

Another spurious prophecy appears in *Doctrine and Covenants*, section 114:1:

> Verily thus saith the Lord: It is wisdom in my servant David W. Patten, that he settle up all his business as soon as he possibly can, and make a disposition of his merchandise, that he may perform a mission unto me next spring, in company with others, even twelve including himself, to testify of my name and bear glad tidings unto all the world.

This prophecy was given April 17, 1838. On October 25, 1838, David Patten was shot and he died. The prophecy was simply false. God, who knows the future, would not call a man to go on a mission, have it predicted and recorded, when he knew that the man would die before the time of the mission came.

One of the oddest and most foolish of all the prophecies was in reference to Oliver B. Huntington, and is recorded both in his diary kept in the Utah State Historical Society and in the Huntington Library in San Marino, California. It was also recorded in the Mormon's *Young Women's Journal*, Volume 3, No. 6 of 1892.

> In my Patriarchal blessing, given by the father of Joseph the Prophet, in Kirtland, 1837, I was told that I should preach the gospel before I was 21 years of

age; that I should preach the gospel to the inhabitants upon the islands of the sea, and to the inhabitants of the moon, even the planet you can now behold with your eyes. The first two promises have been fulfilled, and the latter may be verified. From the verification of the two promises we may reasonably expect the third to be fulfilled also.

When all of this is put together with Apostle Parley Pratt's prophecy in 1838 that in 50 years there would not be an unbelieving Gentile upon this continent, and with Heber C. Kimball's prophecy that Brigham Young would become President of the United States, the case in favor of Mormon prophecy is hopeless. History itself judges Mormon prophecy to be false and baseless. This conclusion is clear without even bothering to consider some of Joseph Smith's infamously false predictions, such as that the New Jerusalem and its temple would be built in Missouri in "this" generation (note *Doctrine and Covenants*, 1832). Heber C. Kimball, member of the First Presidency thirty-nine years later, was still trying desperately to believe the prophet's words. He said, "This generation has not passed away; but before they do pass away this will be fulfilled" (*Journal of Discourses*, volume 15, page 275). One hundred and forty-six years later we still cannot find the New Jerusalem anywhere in Missouri!

Foolishly, desperately, hopelessly, some Mormons have tried to salvage the honor of their prophet by claiming that a biblical prophet, Jonah, also gave a false prophecy when he said that the people of Nineveh would be overthrown with their city. Nineveh was not destroyed, however. The people repented. Perhaps, Mormons say, some of Joseph Smith's prophecies were conditional also.

But Mormons have not looked closely at Jonah's prophecy. Jonah said, first, that Nineveh was to be overthrown because of its wickedness (Jonah 1:2). Then God warned them through Jonah that they had forty days to repent. And finally repentance postponed the destruction of Nineveh. The full prophecy was, "Nineveh, because of wickedness, will be overthrown in forty days." Nineveh repented, the wickedness was eliminated, and the city was spared. Even Jonah was disappointed, since the wickedness made him angry. So the Jonah story provides no precedent for erroneous and spurious prophecies.

Other Mormons say, "But the prophets of the Bible had their faults too." But the point is that when a prophet spoke for God, no matter what his faults might have been, his prophecies had to come true or he was regarded as a false prophet.

The case is clear: Mormon prophecies are inaccurate, misleading, false, completely unbiblical. The fruits of Mormonism are contradictions and revelations of convenience.

Chapter 6

Revelation and the Mormon Mind

An appalling effect of Mormon revelation is that it sears the minds of those who accept it. Even as a branding iron hardens and makes callous the skin that it sears, so the "revelations" of Mormonism make hard and insensitive the minds of Mormon believers. I do not say this disparagingly, but sadly. It is true. Mormon believers simply cannot understand and mentally penetrate the simplest and clearest Bible passages.

Yet a strange thing occurs once a person has accepted Mormon revelation. Difficult passages of scripture, those which godly Christians and great biblical scholars puzzle over, Mormons greet with a quick and ready "interpretation." Their "revelation" gives them a quick and superficial answer to serious problems of interpretation.

But most troubling of all, Mormons invent new meanings for Bible words and phrases. These meanings avoid or distort the clear and simple meanings of scriptural texts. For example, the Broad Way spoken of in Matthew 7:13 in Mormon hands leads to the Terrestrial heaven or the second degree of glory. But the text clearly says that it leads to destruction—to hell. How can destruction be equated with heaven?

Mormons also teach that to be damned means simply "to clog up," as in clogging up a sink drain. Believers are damned when they clog up the flow of God's blessing. Yet, in scripture the word "damned" is often used interchangeably with the word "condemned." It is used as the opposite of being saved. One is saved to go to heaven; one is damned to go to hell.

Mormons also attempt to redefine the word "eternal." A Mormon leader in the special group of "Seventy" wrote to me concerning the phrase which says that God exists "from everlasting to everlasting." He said that this does not mean that God was always God from all time, but that "from everlasting to everlasting" means only from before the beginning of time until after the end of time. He illustrated it this way:

Everlasting   TIME   Everlasting

My friend wants me to believe that this means that from some period before time began until some period after time ends, God is God. But this is a peculiar way of thinking. We must believe that when God speaks to mankind, He uses language and terminology mankind can understand. Thus the clear and simple meaning of biblical references to God's life in time is that "There was never a time from forever past that I was not God. I always have been God, I am God now, and I will forever be God in the future, time or no time."

Isaiah 43:10 puts the lid on any attempt of Mormon teachers to suggest that God was a man before He rose to Godhood. It says, "Before me, there was no God formed, neither shall there be after me." When confronted with this clear statement, many Mormons say that there was a God before this God from which man-who-became-God came, and so on *ad infinitum*. But scripture plainly states that God always existed as the one and only God.

Because the Mormons also want to deny the fact of eternal hell, they have tampered with the word "eternal" in reference to hell. For instance, one writer told me,

> When you read of "eternal punishment," this doesn't mean the punishment will last forever; it means that "eternal" (one of God's titles) is God's name. God is the one who has no end. To receive punishment by God (The Eternal One) is receiving "eternal punishment."

This appears to be a strange way of speaking. If McElveen is administering punishment to his son, the punishment would be "McElveen punishment." Then of course, there would also be in my son's vocabulary "Principal punishment," if he were to misbehave at school, or "teacher punishment," if the misbehavior were in the classroom. This is indeed a strange way to put things. But if eternal punishment doesn't mean that punishment will last forever, how can we read of eternal life and think of it to mean life that will last forever? The exact same work, *Aionios,* is used for the duration of God. If one is translated "eternal," then it would seem that in all cases it should be translated as "eternal." If God is eternal, if heaven is eternal, then so is hell.

The teaching of Mormonism leans always toward this semantic sophistry that has no consistent basis in either scripture or common sense. But to me the most heartbreaking and disturbing sign of what Mormonism does to Mormon minds is what occurs when I show a Mormon friend a simple verse such as Romans 10:13, which says, "For whosoever shall call upon the name of the Lord shall be saved." Most

Mormons simply cannot understand such a promise. To simply *believe* and to *call* upon the Lord for salvation is too difficult to accept.

The same is true if I show a Mormon Romans 4:1-5, where it says that Abraham and David were counted righteous, justified before God, simply by believing, apart from any good works they might have done. In fact, that section of scripture says that it was to those who "worketh not, but believeth on him that justifieth the ungodly, his faith is counted for righteousness." Those who work, in any degree or in any way, for their salvation, were not accepted and were counted as in debt to God.

One Mormon friend sent me a study by Mormon Apostle Orson Pratt on this passage. The study is a classic in misunderstanding. Pratt contends that this verse refers to such works as circumcision, and is not intended to cover all kinds of works that people could do to please God and make themselves worthy of salvation.

But Pratt forgets that David and Abraham both are used as examples in the passage. Both were saved by believing only, according to the passage, totally apart from any works whatsoever that they might have done! No works of any kind were required—biblical, Christian, or Mormon works. If no works were good enough to save Abraham or David, what works or ceremonies does a Mormon think would be good enough to save him?

To make sure no one would be deceived by such circuitous reasoning as Mormons give, in other contexts God gave such simple verses as "Believe on the Lord Jesus Christ and thou shalt be saved." Or "For by grace are ye saved through faith, and that not of yourselves, it is the gift of God. Not of works, lest any man should boast" (Ephesians 2:8, 9). Notice too, that scripture declares that Christ died for the ungodly, and He justifies the ungodly. This has been a stumbling block for self-righteous people ever since it was first stated. And clean-living Mormons continue to stumble over it.

But scripture also says that faith without works is dead. That means that heart belief, saving faith, always produces good works *after* salvation. Salvation that is not demonstrated does not exist, so the saved always show forth their salvation. Most conclusively we must admit that we cannot show forth what we do not already have!

Mormons simply do not understand instant salvation, in spite of numerous examples and promises given in scripture. Everyone is either saved or lost at this moment in time. I was saved on September 29, 1949, at about 2:30 in the afternoon. I knew it then and I know it now. The joy and peace that flooded my heart is still fresh as a memory and a living experience. The Word of God was my assurance, and the Spirit of God witnessed to my spirit. My feelings of joy and peace followed after my experience. Feelings or good works were not the grounds for my salvation. However, after Jesus saved me, *He* changed my life.

But notice this quote from a Mormon friend:

> "But as many as received him, to them gave he power to become the sons of God, even to them that believe on his name" (John 1:12). When one believes on his name, power is given to him *to become* a son of God. He doesn't get it all at once.

But my Mormon friend is confused. And most Mormons are confused on this issue of being a child of God. Most of them teach that we are at birth children of God (even though John 8:44 and I John 3 say that unsaved people are children of the devil). Other Mormons teach that one is born again upon baptism. But that is only a partial rebirth as a child of God, apparently. Because Mormons want to believe that one must gradually progress into sonship with God.

Yet scripture teaches that we become sons of God the moment we receive Jesus Christ. That this is true can be seen from many scriptural passages. Note John 1:13, "Who were born [past tense], not of blood, nor of the will of the flesh, nor of the will of man, but of God." Then consider I John 3:2, which speaks of those who had accepted Christ, "Beloved, now are we the sons of God; therefore, the world knoweth us not, because it knew him not."

We do indeed "get it all at once." There certainly is growth in grace. But that is another subject entirely.

I cannot imagine any of the Israelites, when God told them to offer a lamb without blemish or spot, pointing to its blood and wondering whether or not it was enough. Can you imagine them adding some fruit to the sacrificial offering? Or worse yet, to add a little perfume or a list of good works to be sure the offering was enough? Yet this is what Mormonism attempts to do! They want to add a little human effort to God's act of reconciliation and forgiveness. But they do not know that human work for salvation nullifies God's grace. Work for salvation is an insult to the sacrifice of Christ. It is saying that a person does not believe that Christ was enough. It is a rejection of the sacrifice of the lamb of God!

Jesus said to a harlot (Luke 7:50) after one short encounter (minus baptism or requirements of good deeds or even a changed life): "Thy faith hath saved thee; go in peace." He used the past tense! She was saved already! She did not have to guess about it, hope for it or be uncertain in any way. God gave His word. Mormons cannot understand this simplicity. And even when they accept it as a scriptural statement, they soon qualify it with some explanation.

What happens to Mormon minds is that the "revelation" prevents them from accepting salvation on God's terms. Something happens to the minds of Mormon believers. They cannot understand simple words and phrases. They cannot accept the simple declaration that "by grace are ye saved through faith."

Mormons also do not accept or recognize as damning to their faith the original copy of an 1826 trial in which Joseph Smith is convicted of deceiving Josiah Stowell, an old man, about finding hidden treasure on his land with a peepstone. The trial occurred six years after Joseph's first vision, the one which serves as the foundation for Mormon faith. They choose to believe, as one Mormon lady told me, "If Brigham Young said the sun was inhabited, then it is." That is, Mormons are able to close their minds to legal evidence, scientific evidence, and scriptural evidence and hold on to the absurd revelations of fraudulent prophets.

Mormons continue to ignore the testimony of former Mormon priest and Egyptologist Dee Jay Nelson as well as some of the world's leading Egyptologists when they show that Joseph Smith did not translate the *Book of Abraham* from Egyptian. They also refuse to accept the testimony of leading archeologists that there is no evidence in America—North, Central, or South—for the claims made by the *Book of Mormon*.

So why write a book such as this? If Mormons refuse to recognize and accept the truth about their religious commitment to spurious revelations, why bother to attempt to change their minds? A telephone call I received about two weeks ago gives the answer. When I answered the ringing telephone, a lady spoke:

"Is this Pastor Floyd C. McElveen?"

"Yes, it is."

"I'm going to cry!" Then I heard a few moments of sobbing.

"Mr. McElveen, I am a Mormon. My husband is a Roman Catholic. We just got through reading your book, *Will the "Saints" Go Marching In?* Both of us asked the Lord Jesus Christ to come into our hearts and lives. Now we know that we are saved. We are so very, very happy. We wanted you to know. Thank you so much!"

So, when I say that Mormon "revelation" darkens and sears the minds of Mormon believers, I must qualify my statement somewhat. There are those Mormons who are seeking, questioning, praying, and wanting to meet Jesus Christ. For those I continue to write, to speak and to pray.

Chapter 7

God Loves Mormons

I. THE MORMON GOD

God loves you and wants you to know that the Mormon's God is NOT the God of the Bible.

A. The Mormon God was once a man. "God Himself was once as we are now, and is an exalted man."—Teachings of Prophet Joseph Smith, p. 345.

B. The Mormon God rose in the "scale of progress" from man to God. (This makes men actually prior to and the creator of God!)

"Remember that God our heavenly Father was perhaps once a child, and mortal like we are, and rose step by step in the scale of progress in the school of advancement; has moved forward and overcome until He has arrived at the point where He now is."

C. Mormonism believes that there are many gods, not just one God.

"And the *Gods* ordered, saying: let the waters under the heaven be gathered together unto one place, and let the earth come up dry; and it was so as they ordered; and the *Gods* pronounced the dry land earth; and the gathering together of the waters pronounced they, great waters; and the *Gods* saw that they were obeyed."—*Pearl of Great Price*, Abraham 4:9-10.

D. Mormon leaders even teach that there is a MOTHER GOD. In the Mormon book *Gospel through the Ages*, p. 98, Mormon author, Milton R. Hunter, said, "The stupendous truth of the existence of a Heavenly Mother, as well as a Heavenly Father, became established facts in Mormon theology."

E. Mormons teach that men may become gods.

"As man is, God once was; as God is man may be."— Articles of Faith, p. 430.

II. THE BIBLICAL GOD

God loves you and wants you to know that there is only *one God.* This *one God* created and is Lord over all the universe, stars, planets and all.

"In the beginning GOD created the heaven and the earth."—Genesis 1:1. (See also John 1:3.)

"Before me there was *no God formed*, neither shall there be after me."—Isaiah 43:10b. God was NEVER a man, and man will NEVER be God!

"From everlasting [that's eternity past] to everlasting [that's eternity future], *thou art God!*"—Psalm 90:2b. God never progressed, earned or attained His way to being God; HE ALWAYS WAS GOD. (The Bible mentions *false* gods, but to believe that other gods really exist is pagan polytheism, not Christianity.)

Clearly, there is not now, and *never* will be, any other God on this planet or any other "world" or planet. There is forever only ONE God.

III. THE MORMON CHRIST

God loves you and wants you to know that the Mormon's Jesus is *not* the Jesus of the Bible.

A. Mormons teach: "Christ* the Word, the First-born, had of course *attained* [worked, progressed, earned] unto the status of Godhead while yet in pre-existence." Obviously, Mormons believe that there was a time when Jesus Christ was *not* God. The Bible teaches that Jesus Christ always was, is now, and forever shall be, God.

Some reliable Mormon sources, such as Apostle Orson Hyde in *Journal of Discourses*, Vol. 4, p. 259-60, teach that Jesus Christ was married and a polygamist. This, of course, has no scriptural basis.

IV. THE BIBLICAL CHRIST

There is one Saviour, Jesus Christ, who is the eternal God.

"For unto us a child is born, unto us a son is given: and the government shall be upon his shoulder: and his name shall be called Wonderful, Counsellor, *The mighty God, The everlasting Father,* The Prince of Peace."—Isaiah 9:6.

Within the nature of God there are three eternal distinctions: God the Father, God the Son, and God the Holy Spirit, and there is only *one* God. Since Jesus is repeatedly called God, we must accept Him as God, or we accept another Jesus. In the Bible, "the Word" means Jesus: "In the beginning was the *Word*, and the *Word* was with God, and *the Word was God!*"—John 1:14. "Beginning" here simply means "from all time." As God was God *from all time*, so was Jesus Christ God—from the beginning, from all

---

*"What Mormons Think of Christ," p. 36.

time! Jesus never progressed, worked, or attained His way into being God. *He always was God.*

God forbade forever the worship of any other God (Exodus 34:14), yet Jesus accepted worship as God on many occasions. "And as they went to tell his disciples, behold, Jesus met them, saying, All hail. And they came and held him by the feet, and *worshipped him!*"—Matthew 28:9.

V. JOSEPH SMITH NOT A PROPHET OF GOD

God loves you and wants you to know that Joseph Smith was NOT a prophet of God.

God's test for a true prophet of God: 100% accuracy in fulfillment, *all* the time in *every* detail of the prophecies given.

"But the prophet, which shall presume to speak a word in my name, which I have not commanded him to speak, or that shall speak in the name of other gods, even that prophet shall die. And if thou say in thine heart, How shall we know the word which the Lord hath not spoken? When a prophet speaketh in the name of the Lord, if the thing follow not, nor come to pass, that is the thing which the Lord *hath not spoken*, but the prophet hath spoken it presumptuously: thou shalt not be afraid of him."—Deuteronomy 18:20-22.

Joseph Smith's prophecies. In *Doctrine and Covenants* 84:1-5, given September 1832, New Jerusalem and its Temple are to be built in Missouri in *this* generation. (According to Mormons this meant at the Temple Lot in Independence, Missouri.) Concerning this clear and definite prophecy, Mormon Apostle Orson Pratt stated, on May 5, 1870, just about what other Mormon leaders also said (*Journal of Discourses*, vol. 9, p. 71: vol. 10; p. 344; vol. 13, p. 326; and vol. 17, p. 111), "The Latter-Day Saints just as much expect to see a fulfillment of that promise during the generation that was in existence in 1832 as they expect that the sun will rise and set tomorrow. Why? Because God cannot lie. He will fulfill all His promises." This prophecy was NOT fulfilled and is *false.*

In *Doctrine and Covenants* 124:56-60, Nauvoo House was to belong to the Smith family forever. Smith was killed in 1844, the LDS (Mormons) were driven from Nauvoo, and the house no longer belonged to the Smith family. This prophecy was *false.*

Doctrine and Covenants, section 97: Zion, Missouri, cannot fall or be moved. *False.* It *did* fall, and it *was* moved.

Book of Mormon, Helaman 14:20, 29: Darkness said to cover the earth for three days at the time of the crucifixion of Christ. *False.* The Bible says darkness lasted only three hours (Matthew 27:45, Mark 15:33 and Luke 23:44).

In 1835, *History of the Church*, vol. 2, p. 182, President-Prophet Smith stated, ". . . the coming of the Lord, which was nigh . . . even 56 years should wind up the scene." *False.*

These are only a selected few of many of Joseph Smith's false prophecies. One such would forever disqualify him as a prophet of God.

Finally, never realizing that men from earth would someday walk on the moon, Joseph Smith declared, "The inhabitants of the moon are more of a uniform size than the inhabitants of the earth, being about six feet in height. They dress very much like the Quaker style and are quite general in style, of the fashion of dress. They live to be very old; coming generally near a thousand years."—*Journal* of Oliver G. Huntington, a contemporary of Joseph Smith and a devout and dedicated Mormon, vol. 2, p. 166.

Joseph Smith failed the test God gave. He was NOT a prophet of God.

VI. BRIGHAM YOUNG *NOT* A PROPHET OF GOD.

God loves you and wants you to know that Brigham Young was NOT a prophet of God.

Brigham Young said that the *sun* as well as the *moon*, was inhabited!—*Journal of Discourses*, vol. 13, p. 271.

In the *Journal of Discourses*, vol. 1, p. 50-51, Brigham Young declared that "Jesus Christ was NOT begotten by the Holy Ghost." ". . . for that which is conceived in her *is of the Holy Ghost."*—Matthew 1:20. No true prophet of God contradicts the Word of God.

In *Journal of Discourses*, vol. 1, p. 50, Brigham Young said, "When our Father Adam came into the garden of Eden, He came into it with a celestial body, and brought Eve, One of his wives, with him. He helped make and organize this world. He is Michael, the Archangel, the Ancient of Days! about whom men have written and spoken—He is our Father and our God, and the only God with whom we have to do."

Brigham Young might be excommunicated if he taught this Adam-God doctrine in the Mormon church today. Modern Mormons generally deny that Adam was God. To deny the doctrine obviously admits that Brigham Young was not a prophet of God. To accept the doctrine contradicts both the Bible and the *Book of Mormon*. Brigham Young was *not* a prophet of God. All the authority in the world derived from such sources is useless.

VII. MORMON PRIESTS AND GENEALOGIES

God loves you and wants you to know that priests and genealogies are done away with since Jesus came.

In the Bible, the priest's main duty was to offer blood sacrifices pointing to the one true sacrifice of Jesus on the cross. When sacrifices ceased at the cross, the Priesthood ceased. No Official PRIESTHOOD, or Office of the Priest now exists. No official priesthood was ever listed as a part of the New Testament church. Calvary ended that. All Christians are now priests (I Peter 2:9). Only Jesus in the New Testament was ever a priest after the "Order of Melchizedek."—Hebrews 7:17-22. The Old Testament Melchizedek merely pictured Christ, as did the Aaronic priesthood. The picture was fulfilled in the *person.*

Also, only Aaron and his sons and descendants could be priests (Numbers 18:1-7). All true priests were blood-line descendants of Aaron.

Genealogies and records, kept partially as title deeds to property and farms, also proved the prophecies concerning the individuals, tribes and family lines through which the Messiah would come. This gave historical verification and guarded against false claims by false Messiahs.

Genealogies were also excellent sources of proving the blood-line descent of the Aaronic priesthood, so that no false priest, those not true descendants of Aaron, could presume to the priesthood.

After the cross, and the beginning of the New Testament church, God allowed the genealogical records to be *totally destroyed* by the Romans under Titus in 70 A.D. He made it impossible for anyone to prove blood-line descent back to Aaron and thus claim to be an Aaronic priest. Anyone claiming to be an Aaronic priest today is a *false* priest.

To make sure we understood that priests and sacrifices ended at the cross and that genealogies had forever fulfilled their purpose and were *done away with*, God's Word declares, in I Timothy 1:4, "Neither give *heed* to fables and endless *genealogies*, which minister questions, rather than godly edifying which is in *faith:* so do."

Titus 3:9 warns, "But avoid foolish questions, and genealogies, and contentions, and striving about the law; for they are unprofitable and vain."

The priesthood was fulfilled in Christ and abolished. God is through with genealogies, and FORBIDS their use.

VIII. GOOD WORKS CANNOT SAVE OR HELP SAVE.

God loves you and wants you to know that ALL men are lost sinners and *must* be born again.

All men have a sin nature and there is NO general salvation. The Bible says in Romans 3:23: "For all have sinned, and come short of the glory of God." This means we are all lost sinners. Romans 3:10b: "There is none righteous, no, not one."

Sin is going our own way (Isaiah 53:6). It is being the God, manager, boss, lord of our own life. It is being self-centered instead of Christ-centered.

"All our righteousnesses are as filthy rags."—Isaiah 64:6a. Romans 4:4-5: "Now to him that worketh [for salvation] is the reward not reckoned of grace, but of debt. But to him that worketh not, but believeth on him that justifieth the ungodly, his faith is counted for righteousness."

An apple tree is an apple tree; it bears apples. So, we sin *because* we have a sin-nature. Beating the apples off the tree does not change the nature of the tree! So, getting rid of some sins does not change our nature!

Besides, how much *good works* can a *dead* man do? As natural men we are ALL, "DEAD in trespasses and sins."— Ephesians 2:1b.

John 5:24: "Verily, verily, I say unto you, He that heareth my word, and *believeth* on him that sent me, *hath* everlasting life, and shall not come into condemnation [judgment], but *is passed* from death unto life."

IX. WHAT IS REAL, BIBLICAL SALVATION?

A. *Salvation Is a Free Gift*

God loves you and wants you to know salvation is not by works, it is a GIFT. Personally receiving Christ, trusting Him alone to save us, is God's way of salvation.

Romans 6:23: "For the wages of sin is death, but the GIFT of God is eternal life through Jesus Christ our Lord." We cannot make ourselves "worthy" of the grace of God. Salvation is a free gift for the unworthy, the undeserving, which we all are. "Christ died for the ungodly."—Romans 5:6.

Ephesians 2:8, 9: "For by grace are ye saved through *faith*; and that not of yourselves: it is the gift of God: not of works, lest any man should boast."

B. *We Need a New Nature!*

God loves you and wants you to know that there is only *one* way of salvation.

Sin Nature
Sinner

John 3:7: "Ye must be born again." John 1:12 tells us how. "As many as received him to them gave he power to become the sons of God, even to them that believe on his name." Accepting Jesus is the *only* way to be *born again*.

We are not by nature children of God. We must receive Christ in order to become the children of God.

Suppose a pig tried to become a sheep by acting like a sheep. Suppose the pig were clothed in sheep wool, ate sheep feed and even learned to bleat like a sheep. Would that change its pig nature and make it a sheep? Would it matter whether or not the pig was "good" or "bad" by pig standards?

New Nature
Christian

Jesus alone can cleanse us from sin and change our nature. I Peter 2:24: "Who his own self bare our sins in his own body on the tree." Jesus took our place and shed His blood to cleanse us from sin. No amount of "good works" can wash away one sin or change our nature.

SALVATION occurs when we call believingly on Jesus to save us. He then comes into our life and we become children of God with a new nature.

Although salvation is not by works, true salvation always produces a changed life. Christ comes in by personal invitation as Lord and Saviour to change our life and live His life through us.

C. *Salvation Is Instant*

God loves you and wants you to know *salvation is instant*. The moment we repent, turn from our sins to Jesus, He saves us. As the hymn says, "Just as I am without one plea, but that thy blood was shed for me." Christ said to the unbaptized, unsaved thief on the cross (an instant salvation response to the thief's believing call), "Today shalt thou be with me in paradise."—Luke 23:43b. (Same place Paul saw as the Heaven of God, II Corinthians 12:2-4.) Jesus granted salvation for a harlot: "Go thy way, thy faith hath saved thee!"—Luke 7:50b.

Salvation includes accepting Jesus Christ as both Lord (God, Lord, new manager of our life) and Saviour. It involves heart (the ruling, governing, choosing, center of our being) belief. Romans 10:9: "That if thou shalt confess with thy mouth the Lord Jesus [Jesus as Lord], and shalt believe in thine heart that God hath raised him from the dead, thou shalt be saved."

D. *Salvation Is Simple*

God loves you and wants you to know *salvation is simple.*
Romans 10:13: "For whosoever shall call upon the name of
the Lord, shall be saved." "The blood of Jesus Christ, his
[God's] Son, cleanses us from all sin."—I John 1:7.

We must personally call believingly on Jesus to save us.
This is how we receive Him. If we do so call, He *must* save us
or God would be lying, and God *cannot* lie. If Jesus loved us
enough to die in bloody agony to save us, would He then
turn us down when we call on Him? *Of course not!*

God loves you and wants you to be saved. Would you like
to receive Jesus as your Lord and Saviour right now? Here is
a prayer you can pray right now, meaning it with all your
heart:

"Lord Jesus Christ, come into my heart and life. Cleanse
me from all sin by your shed blood. Make me a child of God.
Give me your free gift of everlasting life, and let me know
that I am saved, now and forever. I NOW receive you as my
very own personal Lord and Saviour. In Jesus' name, amen."

Did Jesus save you or did He lie? He *had* to do one or the
other according to Romans 10:13, if you called believingly
on Him. Which did He do?

E. *Salvation Is Certain*

You can *know* you are saved, not just by *feeling*, but because God's Word says so! Memorize John 3:36a: "He that
believeth on the Son HATH everlasting life." What do you
have right now, according to God's Word? Where would you
go if you were to die right now, according to God's Word?

If you now know that Jesus has saved you, according to
His word, please thank Him out loud for saving you as we
pray.

I John 5:13a: "These things have I written unto you that

believe on the name of the Son of God; that ye may KNOW that ye HAVE eternal life."

F. *Salvation Is Believing!*

Choose to believe Christ, feelings or no feelings, and He will prove His reality to you as you step out on faith that He has kept His word and saved you.

Three men step aboard an elevator bound for the third floor where they all want to go. One is laughing, one is crying, one is poker-faced, unemotional. All three of them get to the third floor, regardless of their feelings, because they *believed* and committed themselves to the elevator. So it is with trusting Christ—feelings or no feelings. He will save you instantly and see you through to Heaven.

The reality of your salvation will be shown in your love-response in obeying and following Jesus Christ. John 14:23a: "If a man love me, he WILL [not if, maybe, and or but] keep my words." If you are truly saved, you *will* obey!

Among other things, this means you will come *out* of Mormonism and follow the Biblical Christ!

G. *True Salvation Produces Good Works, Obedience to Christ*

To *work for* salvation shows unbelief in the sufficiency of Jesus Christ alone to save us. However, true salvation, true faith, *always produces* good works!

James 2:20: "But wilt thou know, O vain man, that faith without works is dead."

Apple trees produce apples. True Christians produce good works. Apples are products of the tree and prove that it is an apple tree. In the same way, good works *never produce* a Christian; they merely prove he is one.

II Corinthians 5:17: "Therefore if any man be in Christ, he is a new creature [creation]: old things are passed away;

behold, all things are become new."

We must *have* salvation in order to *demonstrate* it, just as we must have a car before we can demonstrate it!

H. *True Salvation Produces Obedience to Christ—John 14:23*

1. Find a church that makes salvation clear, that believes the Bible, and the Bible *alone*, that believes the blood of Christ alone can cleanse from sin.

2. Attend church *faithfully* (Hebrews 10:25 and I John 3:14).

3. Follow Christ in baptism to picture your sins being washed away, *after* you have been saved (Acts 10:47, 48), and to picture your death with Christ to the old life, and your resurrection with Him to new life, identified with Him.

4. Pray daily (I Thessalonians 5:13, John 15:7).

5. Confess sin instantly (I John 1:9). Though a Christian might fall into sin, a true Christian cannot continue habitually in sin (1 John 3:9).

6. Read the Bible daily (Acts 17:11, I Peter 2:2).

7. Confess Christ publicly (Luke 12:8-9).

8. Share Christ with others constantly (Acts 1:8).

9. Make a clean break with Mormonism. The souls of *others*, as well as your own, depend on it!

Begin memorizing at least a verse a week. Thank God every day that Jesus has saved you and thank Him for all things, good and bad (I Thessalonians 5:18). Obey Him, believe him—feelings or no feelings—by faith. Believe Him for His victory, thank Him and step out on faith and He will prove His victory in your experience.

For further information, write: Pastor Floyd C. McElveen, 749 Orrfelt Drive N.W., Bremerton, Washington 98310. Phone: 206/692-5896.

Appendix I

CORRESPONDENCE BETWEEN PROFESSOR DEE JAY NELSON AND THE CHURCH OF JESUS CHRIST OF LATTER-DAY SAINTS

Attention: First Presidency
Church of Jesus Christ of Latter Day Saints
Church Office Building
Salt Lake City, Utah

This letter is to inform you that it is our considered desire that my own name and those of my wife and daughter be removed from the membership rolls of the Latter-Day Saints Church.

We:

> Dee Jay Nelson
> Katherine G. Nelson (Mrs. Dee Jay Nelson)
> Kim Cherie Nelson

do freely, and with full understanding of the implications of the step, require that our names be removed from all membership records of the L.D.S. Church.

I, Dee Jay Nelson, do hereby renounce and relinquish the priesthood which I now hold.

Following my translation (the first to be published) of the bulk of the hieratic and hieroglyphic Egyptian texts upon the Metropolitan-Joseph Smith Papyri Fragments three of the most eminent Egyptologists now living published corroborating translations. These amply prove the fraudulent nature of the Book of Abraham, in which lies the unjust assertion that negros are unworthy of participation in the highest privileges of the L.D.S. Church.

We do not wish to be associated with a religious organization which teaches lies and adheres to policies so blatantly opposed to the civil and religious rights of some citizens of the United States.

By affixing our signatures to this document we exercise our constitutional rights of religious freedom and separate ourselves from the Church of Jesus Christ of Latter Day Saints.

Dee Jay Nelson
Katherine G. Nelson
Kim Cherie Nelson

Date: Dec. 8, 1975

February 10, 1976

Professor Dee Jay Nelson
719 Highland Park Drive
Billings, MT 59102

Dear Professor Nelson:

A Stake Presidency and High Council court will be convened at the Billings Montana Stake offices at 2929 Belvedere on March 7, 1976 at 7 a.m. with the respect to the attitude of yourself, your wife and daughter toward membership in the Church of Jesus Christ of Latter-Day Saints. It is the desire of this court that you and your family be present and hereby summoned to appear.

If you find it inconvenient to be present at that time, I would be glad to hear from you, so that a new date and time might be established. If I do not hear from you in this re-

gard, or you do not appear at the time as arranged, the court
will be held as scheduled, and will proceed with this matter
on the basis of the information available at that time.

Respectfully,

Robert L. Eardley
Stake President
BILLINGS MONTANA STAKE

cc: Elder Mark E. Petersen
    Bishop Richard Gibbs

Received by registered mail Feb. 12, 1956

February 15, 1976

Mr. R. L. Eardley
2124 Lyman Ave.
Billings, Montana 59102

Dear Mr. Eardley,

Your certified letter of February 10, 1976 was received a
few days ago. We found it offensive, implying by the word
"court" that we were to be judged. The phrase which you
used, "summoned to appear," might better have been word-
ed, "requested to appear" as we are no longer under your
jurisdiction.

My wife, my daughter and I have already resigned from
the L.D.S. Church by formal written notification addressed
to the First Presidency on December 8, 1975.

The scientific world finds the Book of Abraham an insult
to intelligence. Some of the most brilliant and qualified
Egyptologists of our time have labeled it fraudulent upon
the overwhelming evidence of the recently discovered

Metropolitan-Joseph Smith Papyri. No truly qualified Egyptologist has yet supported it.

We do not wish to be associated with a church which teaches lies and racial bigotry.

Sincerely,
Dee Jay Nelson

DJN/gh

Appendix II

A RECENT CONVERT

Joyful Greetings:

How can I tell you of the blessed miracle which has happened to our family? By the marvelous, wonderful grace of God, we have been called out from darkness and redeemed by our precious Lord and Saviour, Jesus Christ. When this was happening to our family, Brenda was at BYU, and you can imagine how she felt about coming home to her apostate Mormon and newly Christian family! There was fear and horror, a strong determination to be strong herself so as not to "fall" and yet her love for her family would not let her abandon us without trying to help. This got her involved with Christians, and she could not withstand the power of God. Brenda herself met Christ—and thus the Father completed in our family what He started. And the miracle continues, for as we each trust in the Lord more and more and give HIM more and more of ourselves, He is able to give us more and more of Himself. For it is His will to conform us to His image: Romans 8:29. And this He does by revealing to us our sins and causing grief because of them, till we are brought to the point of just turning it all over to Him, and letting His power, through faith and prayers, bring about the changes, solve our problems, fulfill our every need and completely work out our lives for us. Now I have a much deeper understanding of Matthew 11:28 than it was ever possible to have before:

> Come unto me, all ye that labour and are heavy laden, and I will give you rest.

also Philippians 4:6:

> Be careful for nothing; but in everything by prayer and supplication with thanksgiving let your requests be made known unto God.

I know what a terrible shock this must be to you, and how I do wish I could speak to you personally, so you might understand how we could not continue to believe in a church which we found to teach the very opposite of what Christ and His apostles taught in the Bible. I would be willing to give my life for the truth, and I don't care how seemingly "good" a church might appear, or how much we love our Mormon friends and would love to continue to fellowship with them; if the *beginnings* and *foundations* of that church are shaky, and the doctrines of that church are not in agreement with the Bible—well, what would we gain to take the easy road in this life, "not rock the boat," but lose our salvation?

Actually, it was not *my* salvation I was so concerned about that started all of this. It was the salvation of two very good Christian friends, whom I felt would surely "see the truth of the Mormon Church" if only they knew of all its wonderful, beautiful, and glorious principles and doctrines. And because talking about Jesus Christ and His gospel was the most important and enjoyable thing in the world to them, I had ample opportunities to really "teach" them about God's "restored gospel." Neither of them knew each other, and it was two completely different encounters, but they both agreed to hear the six missionary lessons (at different times, of course). Needless to say, they didn't "accept" the Mormon gospel; and it's so very strange, but as I look back now, I guess I didn't hear a word they said because I thought, at the time, they were just "bullheaded," and that if we talk about it long enough they would eventually "come to see the truth." This led each of them and myself to study the Bible in depth as we tried to answer each other's questions. I soon came to realize that even though I was very familiar with Mormon doctrine, *they* had a much greater understanding of the Bible than I did. Everytime I used one of the Bible scriptures the Mormons use to try to prove a doctrine, I was now forced to read the scriptures *before* and *after*, and in fact, the whole Book to see what it was really saying. Time and again I was amazed! But, why should that have bothered me? you say. After all, as a Mormon I should have known that the Bible is not necessarily all true as we have it today—that's one reason why we need a "living Prophet." And that argument worked just fine for me until I started reading the Bible (several versions) and found so *many* verses telling us that we *can* rely on the Bible. Gradually (I didn't even realize it was happening) as I continued to read God's Word, I came under conviction by the Holy Spirit that His Word was perfect in doctrine and in the saving knowledge of Jesus Christ, and that I not only *could* rely on it, but that I *must* rely on it if my family and I were to have eternal salvation. I don't know exactly when it happened, but one day I found that I was horrified at the thought of *some*, that the Bible was merely written by men and not preserved by the Holy Spirit, and thus subject to error. Suddenly it came into sharp forcus—there are two camps (or sides) on this earth. On the first side, we have those who unreservedly uphold the Word of God (Bible), trusting it completely. And on the second side are those who would (and *do*) undermine (sometimes subtly) the Bible and proclaim that the Bible is not a supernatural book. Instead they believe their own intellectual ideas or scientific knowledge—(Atheists), or NEW prophets and scriptures—(Spiritualists, Jehovah's Witnesses, Mormons, Bahai, Science and Mind, etc.), are to be trusted over the Bible. Well, why not, you say? I can only tell you why not for me. First, please notice that there are many groups in the second camp, but there is only one group in the first—BORN-AGAIN CHRISTIANS, who feel there is no salvation in any particular denomination, or in following a prophet, or Pope, etc., but only in and through Jesus Christ. And "Jesus Christ and Him crucified" *only* do they preach. These Christians all belong to the same church—the CHURCH OF JESUS CHRIST, even though they fellowship in many different denominations and church buildings, oftentimes with many non-Christians who also attend these buildings for various other reasons—such as the same reasons people join fraternities, or because of the good programs for their youth, or for social reasons. But, back to the two camps. You know the saying, "birds of a feather will flock together." And there I was (as a Mormon) in the same camp with the atheists and all the other cults, who didn't believe in the sufficiency or accuracy of the Bible. To me it was a glaring revelation. It also hit me with a very sharp impact that when a person, an organization, a church, or whatever, takes the position that the Bible is not preserved by the Holy Spirit, they have *lost* their complete foundation and criteria for truth! How can you *know* if the Mormon prophet is from God if you don't have a reliable guide from which to judge whether he is preaching the same or "ANOTHER GOS-

PEL"? Don't you see how this opens the way for Satan to come as an "angel of light" and teach you *anything he wants?* Just *think* of it! He has free reins. No longer do the teachings you receive from (what you think is) God have to agree with the *only reliable criteria* we have of what Christ taught—the Bible. That is why Satan has so very cleverly attacked the Bible. He knows it is the "sword of the spirit" (Eph. 6:17). It is the very tool God has given us to fight Satan's clever ploys. And so, of course, he has to remove it as a threat, first of all. In the Mormon church he has managed to completely flip things around. Now, instead of checking new prophets and new revelations with the Bible to see if they agree, the Mormons now check out the *Bible* to see if any particular verse in the Bible is correct according to the new revelations.

From Orson Pratt's pamphlet entitled "Divine Authenticity of the Book of Mormon" on pages 45 and 47 we read:

> If it be admitted that the apostles and evangelists did write books of the New Testament, that does not prove of itself that they were divinely inspired at the time they wrote. . . . Add all this imperfection to the uncertainty of the translation, and who, in his right mind could for one moment suppose the Bible in its present form to be a perfect guide? Who knows that even one verse of the Bible has escaped pollution, so as to convey the same sense now that it did in the original?

Wow! What a coup that was. So now, this is what we have according to Mormons. A person can find out if the Mormon Church is true by reading the Book of Mormon and letting the Holy Spirit testify of its truthfulness to you, right? Well, that would be a perfect way to find out—IF the only spirit in this world was the *HOLY* Spirit. Unfortunately, as we all know, there is another power exceedingly powerful and active in this world today. And his every move and inspiration is calculated to keep people away from a saving knowledge of Jesus Christ.

The Gospel of Jesus Christ is the same now as it was when Jesus and Peter and Paul were preaching it. Please stick to the Bible, God's Holy Word. If a spirit or a man teaches you that something different is from God, please know *that* spirit is not from God. God did not leave us alone in this world to try to determine where inspiration or revelation is coming from. He knew that there would be many false prophets, and that we'd have to have a way of knowing, besides our own unreliable feelings. And thus He has given us His Word as a testimony and witness which will stand forever. I realize this letter is long but please bear with me, as we are considering the most important question of your life.

I think it would be important now to include here some of the verses from the Bible which teach that you can rely on it completely for proof and justification of the Holy Spirit's teaching. First, let us read II Peter 1:20, 21:

> Knowing this first, that no prophecy of the scripture is of any private interpretation. For the prophecy came not in old times by the will of man: but holy men of God spake as they were moved by the Holy Ghost.

This teaches us that these men did not *write* as they privately or personally believed (v. 20), but rather as the Holy Ghost moved them (v. 21). So the Holy Ghost actually wrote the prophecy of the scripture through the instrumentality of human hands. Then in II Timothy 3:16 we read:

> All scripture is given by inspiration of God, and is profitable for doctrine, for reproof, for correction, for instruction in righteousness.

So now we know that *all* scripture is given by inspiration of God. So, if the Holy Ghost wrote the Bible, He would certainly preserve it. In fact, read what the Word of God says about its durability:

> Isaiah 40:8: The grass withereth, the flower fadeth: but the word of our God shall stand *forever*..

> Matthew 24:35: Heaven and earth shall pass away, but my words shall *not* pass away.

Wow! Think how *durable* is the Word of God. More durable than heaven and earth! Yet the Mormons believe that God allowed man to mess up important doctrines in the Bible, and that many "plain and precious truths" have been removed. Thus we need the *Book of Mormon*. However, the *Book of Mormon* seems *also* to be missing many "plain and precious truths": (1) Pre-existence, (2) Genealogies, (3) Baptism for the dead, (4) Celestial Marriage, (5) Three degrees of glory, (6) Godhood promised to men, (7) Temporary hell, (8) Eternal Progression. . . . . The *Book of Mormon* is supposed to contain a *"fullness* of the everlasting gospel," but if these things were taken out of Mormonism today, you would certainly *not* have the same Mormon gospel.

The Article of Faith the Mormon Church uses to explain their viewpoint of the Bible is, "We believe the Bible to be the Word of God as far as it is translated correctly." Now if an unknowing Christian were to read that, they would think that sounds pretty much the way they believe it, because after all, it's the Christians who go back to the original Greek and Hebrew to check on the translation. However, it should be noted here that what the Mormons mean by this is far different from the way it sounds. They believe there are many paragraphs and whole books missing from the Bible. They do not believe the Holy Spirit preserved the Bible as an accurate reliable picture and witness of what

Christ taught while upon the earth. Imagine it! And yet in Luke 24:27, 44-46 we have an account of Jesus Himself using the Old Testament as an accurate witness. If it were wrong, He would have *told them*! Which brings up an interesting question. Why did not the next prophet, or any prophet after Joseph Smith, finish revising the Bible by revelation as God supposedly directed Joseph Smith to do? It seems strange that He would allow such an important assignment to go unfinished when He had a perfectly good prophet at all times after Joseph Smith died.

I would now like to deal a little with the subject of the "great apostasy," or "falling away." Was there indeed a need of a restoration of Christ's Church upon the earth, and do we need a "prophet to guide us in these latter days"?

Matthew 16:18: I will build my church; and the gates of hell shall *not* prevail against it.

Matthew 28:20: And, lo, I am with you alway, even unto the end of the world. Amen.

Here Christ says that hell would *NOT* prevail against His Church, and the very last thing that Jesus said to His followers before He ascended was that He was *always* going to be with them (that means without interruption) till the end of the world! Just whom did He mean He was going to be with if there were not going to *be* any Christians or Church shortly after He died? It's true there would be a "falling away," and there *has* been a great falling away, and it still goes on. There are many apostate churches in the Christian world today who have not steadfastly clung to the faith. But there has always been a *remnant*; that is obvious by what has been quoted from Matthew. So if hell did *not* prevail and a remnant of the Church has always been here, is the need for a modern day prophet a true doctrine?

In fact, you might have thought when I quoted II Timothy 3:16 previously, that "all scripture" would include latter-day revelations too, but because of what Hebrews 1:1, 2 and Jude 1:3 say, we know "all scripture" cannot include material which was not written and taught at the time of Christ.

> Hebrews 1:1, 2: God, who at sundry times and in divers manners spake *in time past* unto the fathers by the *prophets, hath in these last days spoken unto us by his Son. . . .*

Here Paul is making a differentiation between the way God spoke in times past and in the way He speaks in these *last* days. *Before* Christ, it was by a prophet and now it is by His Son, whose words are recorded in the Bible.

> Jude 1:3: Ye should earnestly contend *for the faith which was once* delivered unto the saints.

Also consider:

> Romans 15:19: I have *fully* preached the gospel of Christ.
>
> I Timothy 1:3, 4: That thou mightest charge some that they teach *no other doctrine*, neither give heed to fables and endless *genealogies*.

Now if God still speaks in these last days through a prophet, the prophet's words have to be the *same doctrine* as in the Bible. And as Paul has "fully" preached the gospel, how *can* there be *new* doctrine? And if there can be no new doctrine, why the need of a prophet with new doctrine? In fact, I know you must realize that in the Book of Revelation, everything is foretold that is going to happen right up to the very moment of our Lord's return. If you take the position that Paul and the apostles *did* have all the Mormon doctrines and it is all just being restored, please read 1 Corinthians chapter 7.

Try to imagine one of your apostles *today* speaking about marriage as if it were not necessary, as Paul was doing. And yet, I have heard Mormon missionaries explain: yes, Paul did know about the necessity of temple marriage. Remember also what the Bible says about its durability.

But, you say, the Mormon Church *can't* be wrong, look at their wonderful organization, the good people (nobody ever had better bishops or friends than we did), the wonderful choir, etc... They even have the right name. (See note at end of letter concerning the name.) Well, my dear friends, just what would be the purpose of a wrong church if not to deceive? If someone was going to make counterfeit money, would they use red ink? And I am referring to Satan as the deceiver, not the Mormon people. As in any question we might have, the Bible will give us the answer to the question, "Could a false church appear righteous?"

> II Corinthians 11:13-15: For such are false apostles, deceitful workers, transforming themselves into the apostles of Christ. And no marvel; for Satan himself is transformed into an angel of light. Therefore it is *no great thing if his ministers also be transformed as the ministers of righteousness*; whose end shall be according to their works.

Also, we *cannot* even rely on great works of miracles to prove we are in the true church. For in Matthew 7:22-23 it says:

> Many will say to me in that day, Lord, Lord, have we not prophesied in thy name? and in thy name have cast out devils? and in thy name done many wonderful works? And then will I profess unto them, I never knew you: depart from me, ye that work iniquity.

So what is there *left* for us to rely on to know truth from error, and to be able to recognize a false prophet if we hear one? The answer is in Galatians 1:8-9:

> But though we, or an angel from heaven, preach any other gospel unto you than that which we have preached unto you, let him be accursed. As we said before, so say I now again, If any *man preach any other gospel* unto you than that ye have received, let him be accursed.

And just how is a person to *know* if a man or an angel *is* preaching another gospel? Jesus tells us to search the Scriptures to see if it be so. Now, would He tell us to search the Scriptures if we could not rely on them? Please consider that question seriously, especially if you are inclined to say as one dear Mormon lady told me today, "I will take what a living prophet of God says *over* the scriptures any day." My dear, if what this living prophet says is *different* than the Scriptures (and it *must* be if you have to "take it *over* the Scriptures") according to Galatians 1:8 (quoted above), he *cannot* be a prophet of God. It's that simple!

So I would like to share with you now just a few of the many doctrines in the Mormon Church which I found to be "another gospel." There are so many beautiful things we have learned from the Bible and through His Spirit, but I realize that in this letter, I will only be able to touch on a very few.

Very basic, of course, would be—God. So that we may have a basis for comparison, let us look at what Joseph Smith taught:

> "and that he was once a man like us: yea, that God himself, the father of us all, dwelt on an earth, the same as *Jesus Christ himself* did:" (from the *King Rollett Discourse*, p. 9)
>
> also
>
> "God himself was once as *we are now*, and is an exalted man, and sits enthroned in yonder heavens: that is the great secret."
>
> and

"And you have got to learn how to be gods your-selves." p. 10

and

"For I am going to tell you how God came to be God, we have *imagined* and *supposed* that God was God from all eternity. I will *refute* that idea, and take away the veil, so that you may see." p. 9

and

"As man is, God once was; as God is, man may be." (*Articles of Faith*, p. 430)

Now would somebody please tell me how the following verses could possibly be the same gospel?

Isaiah 43:10, 11: I am he: before me there was no God formed, neither shall there be after me. I, even I, am the Lord: and beside me there is no saviour.

Isaiah 44:6: Thus saith the Lord the king of Israel, and his redeemer the Lord of hosts; I am the first, and I am the last: and beside me there is no God.

Isaiah 44:8: Is there a God beside me? yea, there is no God; I know not any.

Isaiah 45:5: I am the Lord, and there is none else, there is no God beside me:

Isaiah 45:21, 22: . . . and there is no God else beside me: a just God and a Saviour: there is none beside me. Look unto me, and be ye saved, all the ends of the earth: for I am God, and there is none else.

Isaiah 46:9: . . . For I am God, and there is none else: I am God, and *there is none like me.*

Psalm 90:2: . . . Even from *everlasting* to *everlasting*, thou art God.

Malachi 3:6: For I am the Lord, *I change not.* . . .

Of course there are many more verses I could quote to prove that *there is only one God*, that He has *always been God*, and has *never changed!*

> I Corinthians 8:6: But to us there is but one God, *the Father*, of whom are all things. . . .

I added that last verse in I Corinthians to point out that Jesus Christ and the Father are *both* referred to as the ONE GOD. This is, of course, because *they* are the ONE GOD. The Holy Spirit or Holy Ghost would also be included, of course:

> For there are three that bear record in heaven, the Father, the Word, and the Holy Ghost: and these three are one.

So, if there is only one God or Godhead, how can *you* become a God? He says He does not even *know* of any others (Isaiah 44:8). Surely, if God was once a man who lived on a planet himself, he would be in close association with many other gods. Yet God adamantly revealed that He doesn't know of *any*! There is only one God! Anyplace! Anytime! He and He only. He is the *creator*, we are the *created*! And the difference lies in our very natures:

> Galatians 4:8: Howbeit then, when ye knew not God, ye did service unto them which *by nature* ARE NO gods.

So we see that God is God *by nature;* and we, my dear friends, are *by nature* human beings, desperately in *need* of God. What a blessing it has been to me to worship the true and living God, the God of the Bible—the God of Abraham, Isaac and Jacob—the ONE self-existent God who has *always been God, and who has never changed* from human to God. What a glorious change from Joseph Smith's god, whom God says exists only in the minds of men. If you believe that God the Father is a "glorified man," please read the following verses:

Hosea 11:9: . . . For I am God, and not man.

Numbers 23:19: God is not a man, that he should lie; neither the son of man, that he should repent.

But Romans 1:23 really brings home just what the Mormons have done:

And *changed* the glory of the uncorruptible God into an image made like to corruptible *man*, and to birds, and four-footed beasts, and creeping things.

Just think, God puts making God into an image like *man*, into the same category as making Him into birds, beasts, etc. What makes this all so frighteningly diabolical is to realize that it was because he wanted to become as God that Lucifer fell:

Isaiah 14:12-15: How art thou fallen from heaven, O Lucifer, son of the morning! How are thou cut down to the ground, which didst weaken the nations! For thou has said in thine heart, I will ascend into heaven, I will exalt my throne above the stars of God: I will sit also upon the mount of the congregation, in the sides of the north; I will ascend above the heights of the clouds: *I will be like the most high.* Yet thou shalt be brought down to hell, to the sides of the pit.

Think of it! Satan, too, aspired to be a God. And that was the sin that caused his downfall!

Another doctrine which really stabbed my heart when I realized fully what it was really saying, was the doctrine called blood atonement. And I believe there are Mormons today who do not even realize that their church teaches such a thing. Christ, in the Bible, says that He died for *all* sin:

I John 1:7: . . . and the blood of Jesus Christ his son cleanseth us from *all* sin.

Now the Mormons come along and say no, Christ did *not* die for all sin:

"But man may commit certain grievous sins—according to his light and knowledge—that will place him beyond the reach of the atoning blood of Christ. If then he would be saved he must make sacrifice of his own life to atone—so far as in his power lies—for that sin, for the blood of Christ alone under certain circumstances will not avail (Doc. of Sal., Vol. I, page 134). (These are writings by Joseph Fielding Smith, compiled by Bruce McConkie.)

and

"Joseph Smith taught that there were certain sins so grievous that man may commit, that they will place the transgressors beyond the power of the atonement of Christ. If these offences are committed, then the blood of Christ will *not* cleanse them from their sins *even though they repent.* Therefore, their only hope is to have their own blood shed to atone, as far as possible, in their behalf. This is scriptural doctrine, and is taught in all the standard works of the Church" (Ibid., p. 135).

What must Christ think when persons make mockery of His atonement by advocating that still further blood atonements are necessary after Christ's LAST and FINAL, and PERFECT atonement? Please also consider the following verses:

Hebrews 10:10: By the which will we are sanctified through the offering of the body of Jesus Christ *once for all.*

Hebrews 10:12: But this man, after he had offered *one sacrifice for sins forever*, sat down on the right hand of God.

Hebrews 10:14: For by *one* offering he hath perfected *forever* them that are sanctified.

These verses of scripture completely refute the Mormon doctrine of blood atonement.

One of the very important doctrines in the Mormon Church is their priesthood or authority. Please read Hebrews 5, 6, and 7. I will quote here 7:23, 24 where it tells that in the Aaronic priesthood (which the Jews had before Christ came) it was necessary to have many priests because they died, (v. 23), but now (v. 24) Jesus, because He does not die, has a Priesthood which does not change from person to person:

> And they truly were many priests, because they were not suffered to continue by reason of death: but this man, because he continueth ever, hath an *unchangeable* priesthood.

The word UNCHANGEABLE here in the original text means UNTRANSMITTABLE. That is obvious from the context as it reads even in the King James version, but just thought I'd mention it so there would be no question about it. So you see, Christ is our HIGH PRIEST, our ONLY HIGH PRIEST after the order of Melchizedek; and the Aaronic priesthood ended with Christ. You never read of any Aaronic Priesthood office ever mentioned in the New Testament. They were *all* members of a "Royal priesthood," and called such offices as pastors, evangelists, deacons, bishops, etc. In fact, the early Christian deacons were obviously men, not boys:

> I Timothy 3:11: Even so must their *wives* be grave, not slanderers, sober, faithful in all things.

So the Mormons don't even have the early Christian usage of deacons. There is so much more that could and should be said about where a Christian gets God's authority to act in His name, but as this already seems to be turning into a book, let it suffice to remind you that a BORN-AGAIN CHRISTIAN has God's Holy Spirit dwelling within him; and with this Holy Spirit comes the authority.

I guess the very core of Christianity we would all have to

agree is the subject of SALVATION—for that is what it's all about. What a revelation it was to me that it is by GRACE that we are saved, and not by our own righteousness:

> Ephesians 2:8, 9: For by grace are ye saved through faith; and that not of yourselves: it is the gift of God: not of works, lest any man should boast.

> Titus 3:5-7: Not by works of righteousness which we have done, but according to his mercy he saved us, by the washing of regeneration, and renewing of the Holy Ghost: which he shed on us abundantly through Jesus Christ our Saviour: that being *justified* by his grace, we should be made heirs according to the hope of eternal life.

> II Timothy 1:9: Who hath saved us, and *called us with an holy calling*, not according to our works, but according to his own purpose and grace, which was given us in Christ Jesus before the world began.

Before we go further, we had better clarify just what the Mormons *mean* if they say they are "saved" by grace. Some will say they are, and others will say not, depending on their understanding of the concept, and whether or not they are familiar with the official position of the church. I will quote from a pamphlet entitled *Constitutions of Joseph Smith*, page 5, by Stephen L. Richards:

> There will be a general salvation for all in the sense in which the term is generally used, but salvation, meaning *resurrection*, is not exaltation.

I would now like to point out that in the Bible, whenever Christ spoke of being SAVED, He was not referring to merely resurrection, but to what the Mormons refer to as "being exalted." Please notice that Christ said *only* those who "believe" would be saved, but we know even those who do not accept Christ will be resurrected—so it follows that He could *not* have been referring to the resurrection. He meant to be saved from spiritual death, INTO God's family and kingdom—or *exalted* (to use a Mormon word) by grace and not works. And as there is only ONE WAY, one road, to Heaven, there can only be one destination (not three). Every other road leads to destruction:

> Matthew 7:13, 15: Enter ye in at the straight gate: for wide is the gate, and broad is the way, that leadeth to *destruction*, and *many* there be which go in thereat: because straight is the gate, and narrow is the way, which leadeth unto life, and *few* there be that find it. Beware of false prophets, which come to you in sheep's clothing, but inwardly they are ravening wolves.

I used to believe that James 2 justified my believing that we were saved (into the Celestial Kingdom) by our good works. However, I have since found that nothing could be further from the truth. James is explaining that it is not just an acknowledgement of who Christ is that will save you, but the type of faith that produces works or fruit that saves. This is further proved by:

> Romans 4:2-8: For if Abraham were justified by works, he hath whereof to glory; *but* not before God. For what saith the scripture? Abraham *believed* God, and it was counted unto him for righteousness. Now to him that worketh is the reward not reckoned of grace, but of debt. But to him that *worketh not*, but *believeth* on him that justifieth the ungodly, his faith is counted for righteousness. Even as David also describeth the blessedness of the man, unto whom God imputeth righteousness *without works*, saying, Blessed are those whose iniquities are forgiven, and whose sins are covered. Blessed is the man to whom the Lord *will not impute sin*.

The ONLY "work" that we are told to do in the Bible is to BELIEVE (repentance is a necessary part of believing) or to have faith in Him and *He* will produce the fruit:

> John 6:28, 29: Then said they unto him, What shall we do, that we might work the works of God? Jesus answered and said unto them, This is the work of God, *that ye believe on him* whom he has sent.

> Acts 16:30-31: And brought them out, and said, Sirs, what must I do to be saved? And they said, *Believe on the Lord Jesus Christ*, and thou shalt be saved, and thy house.

And if you still think it's your works that is going to save you into the Celestial Kingdom, please read:

> Romans 11:5, 6: Even so then at the present time *also* there is a remnant according to the *election of grace*. And if by grace, then is it no more or works: otherwise grace is no more grace. But if it be of works, then is it no more grace: otherwise work is no more work.

Now when I was a Mormon I used to think that the Christians who believed they were saved by grace were given a free license to go out and sin all they wanted to. But I soon found out that it just doesn't work that way. As I mentioned at the beginning of my letter, the Holy Spirit reveals things about yourself you would never know in your natural (before rebirth) state. And not only that, but He gives you the *power* to overcome your sins. How glorious it is to obey the Lord, *not* to gain salvation or exaltation, but just because you love the Lord, and knowing that, because He died for you, your greatest desire in life is to live for Him! That can't compare with the idea of offering our puny works in exchange for exaltation.

This is what "BELIEVING ON JESUS" really means!

It means that we BELIEVE Him when He tells us that the "wages of sin is DEATH," and so if we are going to be punished for our own sins (even one little unrepented sin), that means death—*spiritual death!* BELIEVING ON JESUS means we BELIEVE Him when He tells us He has died and paid IN FULL the penalty for OUR sins and therefore, we will not be punished for our sins! And BELIEVING ON JESUS means that you BELIEVE Him when He tells you that you must ACCEPT HIM AS YOUR (PERSONAL) SAVIOUR. To accept Jesus as your (personal) Saviour means that you accept His DEATH in PAYMENT for all YOUR sins, thereby being granted COMPLETE and FULL EXALTATION—(which is the closest Mormon word we could use to designate the Biblical meaning of the word SALVATION, as explained earlier); and this apart from any works. If I felt that after I had ACCEPTED CHRIST, that *I* still had work to do to gain the Celestial Kingdom, then I *would not have really accepted* Christ's FREE GIFT of SALVATION, THE work of which is *already* done! That is why the last thing Jesus said on the cross was, "It is finished." The *work* of saving men's souls was *finished.* But it still remains for each individual to *accept* that gift by FAITH and TRUST that Christ has died in your place, and thus ACCEPT CHRIST. After you have done this, *He* will come and dwell in you, and *produce the fruits.* You do not produce the fruit and thus you do not have anything in yourself in which to glory. The glory is ALL HIS. Here again, the only thing you do is to, by your will, allow Him to make, mold, and conform you to His image (Romans 8:29). What a fantastic plan; but Satan would like to take the glory away from God, and have us believe that, because Christ died on the cross, now *we* can work our way to Heaven. But God makes it abundantly clear in the Bible that *man cannot* produce good works, as the following verses so clearly testify:

Isaiah 64:6: But we are all as an unclean thing, and all *our* righteousnesses are as filthy rags.

Romans 7:18: For I know that in me (that is, in my flesh) dwelleth no good thing. . . .

THAT IS why we need to be clothed in the RIGHTEOUS-NESS OF CHRIST when we come to the MARRIAGE SUP-PER of CHRIST and His BRIDE (church). Anyone that comes in his own robe will not be allowed admittance. Please read the parable of the Marriage Feast, Matthew 22:1-13. Dear friends, please don't try to get into Heaven in your own righteousness, as the Jews did, for they *too* were very zealous!

Romans 10:2-4: For I bear them record that they have a zeal for God, but not according to knowledge. For they being ignorant of God's righteousness, and going about *to establish their own righteousness*, have not submitted themselves unto the righteousness of God. For Christ is the end of the law for righteousness to everyone that believeth.

Romans 9:31, 32: But Israel, which followed after the law or righteousness, hath *not* attained to the law of righteousness. Wherefore? Because they sought it not by faith, but as it were by the works of the law. For they stumbled at that stumblingstone.

For *Christ* is the WAY into Heaven—not just by following His example, but by actually putting Him *on* and being "IN CHRIST":

Romans 3:22: Even the righteousness of God which is by faith of Jesus Christ *unto* all and *upon* all them that believe:

II Corinthians 5:17: Therefore if any man be *in* Christ, he is a new creature.

As I said earlier, there are many more doctrines and historical evidences which I could mention, but if the possibility of the Mormon Church being false doesn't even enter your mind after reading this—more evidences would not mean anything either. And even as I write this, I realize the impossibility of your truly realizing what all this means until after you have ACCEPTED CHRIST as your PERSONAL SAVIOUR as explained in the little booklet, *Four Spiritual Laws.*

> I Corinthians 2:14: But the natural man receiveth not the things of the Spirit of God: for they are foolishness unto him: neither can he know them, because they are spiritually discerned.

Such was the case with me. It was not until about three days after I accepted Him as my personal Saviour that I *knew* the Mormon church was wrong. So I would exhort you to please read over the little booklet and let the Holy Spirit teach you how to *become His child.* Then, reread this letter, *read the Bible* and watch a miracle happen. And do not be fearful to find out the truth, for it says in Revelation 21:8:

> But the fearful . . . shall have their part in the lake which burneth with fire and brimstone: which is the second death.

Please understand that I am writing this letter for one reason only. It is not because I enjoy tearing down something you love and have faith in. But it grieves me to think that you, *who want so much* to do God's will, have "believed a lie." And I would only ask that you "prove all things." I know that the thought of the Mormon Church being false is so utterly devastating to you, that it's almost impossible to even *begin* to consider it. I know, I was there. But it is just as difficult for a Jehovah's Witness, or a Bahai, or any other cult member to believe that their church is not the only true church, as it is for you. And yet, you *know* their church is not true. So faith in something doesn't make it true. And please remember, it's not the true Church of Jesus Christ that we have *left*, but the true Church of Jesus Christ that we have *found*; and *Christ Himself* has joined us to His Church. Even if you don't believe this, please remember *that we do*, and so what kind of love would we have for you if we did not try to *help you too*?

I feel so much for all of you, and no matter what you might think of us, please know that we love you, and only wish to set you free "IN CHRIST" so that you too may have eternal and everlasting salvation. Please let us hear from you and may the grace of God enfold you.

In His Love and in His Service,
Doug and Janet and kids
Written by Janet Webster

Appendix III

THE CHURCH OF UNCERTAIN NAME

According to the Mormon assertion, Christ "restored" His church using the Mormon prophet, Joseph Smith, as the instrument through whom this was accomplished. The "precise day" for the organization of the church was supposedly revealed, along with the name by which it was to be called. The name given by "divine revelation" was THE CHURCH OF CHRIST. However, four years later, in 1834, the name of the church was changed to THE CHURCH OF THE LATTER DAY SAINTS. Then another four years later, in April of 1838, the name was again changed. This time it became, THE CHURCH OF JESUS CHRIST OF LATTERDAY SAINTS.

Does it not seem strange that it took eight years and three "revelations" to name the "true church"?

(Quoted from the tract "Changes in Mormonism" from Utah Christian Tract Society, P.O. Box 725, LaMesa, Ca. 92041)

Appendix IV

Mormons have begun blitzing the media, TV, *Reader's Digest*, etc., with their polished propaganda. Their focus is on the family. All of us love our families, and recognize the importance of a family unit reflecting God's love. However, Mormons have very nearly idolized the family to a point where even greater spiritual truths are obscured. Even the worship of God and salvation through the Lord Jesus Christ seem to be relatively important only as they feed this focus on the family. Strange it is to discover that Mormon polygamy furnished one of the greatest threats to the family ever posed in America for generations, had it not been overthrown by the U.S. government and convenient Mormon revelation. Strange too, that in Utah—listed as about 75% Mormon now, and some years back, a much higher percentage than that—has had a divorce rate as high as, or higher than, the national average in America, for all but three or four years since 1908! Seems very much like the case of 'whited sepulchers' of which Jesus spoke in reference to some of the religious Pharisees and their claims.

Finally, if Mormonism were true, and men could become 'gods' on separate planets, the vaunted unity of Mormon families, for which they sacrifice so much, would be shattered forever. Good Mormons in the same family, upon becoming 'gods,' would find themselves separated by millions of light years on their individual planets and might never see each other again! God clearly indicated that there will be no marriage or giving in marriage, since we will be in that respect like the angels. Angels do not marry, no angel babies are being produced. Mormonism is a cruel hoax perpetrated upon a people zealous and religious, but lost. God loves Mormons and wants them saved from this delusion, and so do we.

Bibliography

The works of Joseph Smith:

The Book of Mormon. Salt Lake City: The Church of Jesus Christ of Latter-Day Saints. First issued, as divided into chapters and verses with references. By Orson Pratt, 1879.

Doctrine and Covenants of the Church of the Latter Day Saints, carefully selected from the Revelations of God, and compiled by Joseph Smith, Jr., Oliver Cowdery, Sidney Rigdon, Frederick G. Williams. Kirtland, 1835. Salt Lake City: 1921.

The Pearl of Great Price, being a choice selection from the revelations, translations, and narrations of Joseph Smith. Liverpool: F. D. Richards, 1851.

History of the Church of Jesus Christ of Latter-Day Saints, Period I. History of Joseph Smith, the Prophet, by himself. 6 volumes. Salt Lake City: Deseret News, 1902-12.

Other works consulted:

Brodie, Fawn M. *No Man Knows My History. The Life of Joseph Smith.* New York: Alfred A. Knopf, 1946.

Fraser, Gordon H. *Joseph and the Golden Plates.* Eugene, Oregon: Gordon H. Fraser, 1978.

Layton, Melaine, *Mormonism,* an unpublished book.

McElveen, Floyd C. *Will the "Saints" Go Marching In?* Glendale, California: Regal Books, 1977.

McConkie, Bruce R. *Doctrines of Salvation.* Salt Lake City: Bookcraft, Inc., 1954.

_____. *Mormon Doctrine.* Salt Lake City: Bookcraft, Inc., 1966.

Ransom, Ira T. *Visualized Witnessing Notebook,* Sacramento: United Missionary Fellowship, 1975.

Talmage, James E. *A Study of the Articles of Faith.* 42 edition. Salt Lake City: The Church of Jesus Christ of Latter-Day Saints.

Tanner, Jerald and Sandra. *Mormonism—Shadow or Reality?* Salt Lake City, Modern Microfilm Co., 1972.

Tope, Wally. *Maximizing Your Witnesses to Mormons,* an unpublished pamphlet.

Witte, Bob (compiled by). *Where Does It Say That?* Scottsdale, Arizona, Coup, 1978.